# Data Analytics for Beginners

## Practical Guide To Master Data Analytics

TECHWORLD

© 2017

Other Books By

## **<u>TechWorld</u>**

# DevOps Handbook

## A Guide to Implementing DevOps In Your Workplace

DevOps is not just a buzzword. It is a mindset that can pull your companies problems by the root and change the traditional, core beliefs. When the old waterfall methods cannot provide you with the desired outcome, it is time for a total transformation that can get you off the downward spiral.

Teaching you the ultimate ways to start implementing DevOps in order to decrease the deployment time and maximize the profit, this book will show you why some of the world's largest companies have chosen to think DevOps.

# CONTENTS

# Introduction

Businesses—whether startups or incumbents—have always had access to data as long as it's available. And strangely enough, these companies have had serious challenges in harnessing their data into meaningful insights in the last couple of years with the majority of them outsourcing their data analysis functions to expatriates.

Because of skyrocketing volumes of data, today's interest in data analytics is unparalleled. While the previous study centered on a few specific departments, today's analysis has to focus on all the departments of the organization. In particular, the bottom line of enhanced data analytics in these units is improving the performance.

But why now, you may ask?

The global business environment in which the companies are operating from has been changing fast. Really fast! Today's businesses must not only compete to increase their ROI, but they must also face stiff competition from their rivals with limited time to market their services and products. Also, these firms have to put up with the ever-evolving demographics such as the emergence of millennials and web 2.0 technologies.

Amidst all these challenges, data analytics is the only hope for the survival of companies in such business environments. Data analytics generates fact-based and insightful-driven decisions that can help firms manage their strategic, operation and financial performance while creating shareholder value. That's why you can no longer ignore data analytics.

This book has been written to help you understand how data analytics can enable an organization navigates against the turbulences created by challenging and complex business environments. In particular, the book explores all the basics of data analytics and how your business can leverage today's data analytics to promote your bottom line.

# Chapter 1: Overview of Data Analytics

Welcome to the world of data analytics! In this chapter, we'll explore all the concepts behind data analytics that will help you get started. This section will provide with a complete big picture view of data analytics. Let's dive in.

## Foundations of Data Analytics

Today, companies are generating vast amounts of data files. The files are created from multiple sources and exist in different locations across the organization's data storage infrastructure. In some instances, the files can contain structured data which can easily be processed by RDBMSs such as SQL Server, MySQL, and Oracle to generate useful information.

However, in most cases, the files will contain unstructured or semi-structured data in the form of emails, documents and other forms of digital media. Unlike the structured data that can easily be processed, both semi-structured and unstructured data — what is commonly called the big data — are particularly difficult to manipulate. In most cases, the amount of big data created by the organization can not only put a strain on its storage resources but also strain on processing capabilities.

From the storage resource perspective, managing any big data in the organization means locating and removing the files that are:

- Obsolete
- Duplicated
- Non-essential

It takes lots of time and energy to search through each of the storage sizes for data that should be archived or even deleted. When you ignore to archive and delete obsolete, duplicated and non-essential files, they will continue to consume your valuable and limited storage capacity.

From the processing resource perspective, manipulating your data requires the application of appropriate statistical skills that can help you mine useful information for decision making. With proper statistical and computing skills, you can quickly evaluate the current state of you data and take actionable steps to help you retrieve and valuable information while mitigating the risk of compliance-related challenges.

Below are benefits that you stand to achieve when you implement best data analytics practices in your organization:

Below are reasons why you should consider investing in data analytics:

- You'll establish a dialogue with your consumers. Today's customers are tough to understand. Data analytics can allow you to profile their clients for a proper understanding of their needs.
- You'll re-examine your products and improve. Data analytics will provide meaningful customers' perception about your product. These sentiments can help you segment your market based on geographical or time zone requirements.
- You'll be in a position to perform risk analysis with your data. Predictive analysis of your data will enable your firm to data for helpful insights that keep you updated about business environments.
- You'll now generate new revenue streams. You can sell any patterns you obtain from your data to non-personalized large firms and expand your revenue base.

## Getting started

By now, you are asking, "Where should I start to become a professional data analyst?"

Good question.

To become a professional data scientist, below are prerequisites:

- Spreadsheets
- Basic SQL
- Web development

Let's see how these fields are important in data analytics.

## #1: Spreadsheets

Any spreadsheet such as Ms Excel can help you analyze data. In fact, Ms Excel can be regarded as the most all-around business application that you can use for data analysis. Most of the functional specific skills such as data mining, visualization, and statistical applications are provided in Ms Excel. You can begin by learning the fundamental concepts of Ms Excel such as the workbook, worksheets, formula bar and the ribbon.

If you complete the basics, you can now begin to master the essential functions such as sum, average, if, vlookup, date, max and getpivotdata. As you become comfortable with these features, you can now dive deeper into more complex formulas for regression, correlation and chi-square distributions.

## #2: Basic SQL

Ms Excel will provide you with tools for slicing and dicing your data by assuming that you already have the data stored on your computer. It doesn't provide tools for data collection and storage. As you'll learn about seasoned data analysts, the best approach for dealing with data is pulling it directly from its source which Excel doesn't provide.

Relational database management systems (RDBMS) that use Structured Query Language (SQL) supports procedures that can help you collect and manage your database in an efficient manner. To understand the RDBMSs, you should have an excellent mastery of SQL. You can begin by learning the following SQL statements:

- Select
- From
- Where
- Group By
- Having
- Order By

Besides mastering these SQL commands, you should also find out how primary keys, foreign keys, and candidate keys are used in the RDBMSs.

### #3: Basic web development

Oddly enough, web development is a bonus to any data analyst. If you want to work with consumer internet companies such as Microsoft, IBM or Amazon, good internet programming skills in HTML, JavaScript and PHP will help you communicate your results in more effective ways.

# Mathematics and Analysis

The fact is: data analytics is all about numbers. If you enjoy working with numbers and algebraic functions, then data analytics is for you. If you don't love numbers, then it's time to begin developing a positive attitude. You should also be willing to learn new ideas. As a matter of fact, data analytics is ever-changing and fast-paced, thanks to the exponential growth of data and IT capabilities.

# Analysis and Analytics

Even though Analysis and Analytics sound similar in pronunciation, there's an important distinction between the two terms. Analysis can be regarded as the discipline of recognizing the business needs of the organization and determining their solutions. On the other hand, Analytics focuses on data collection, techniques, and skills that can help in the investigation of past business performance.

In particular, the primary role of Analysis is to separate the whole business problem into its parts while analytics provide a logical solution to the problems identified in the organization. When you think regarding the past and future, the analysis looks backward over the time and gives you a historical view of what has happened in the organization while analytics models the future or predict the result.

# Communicating Data Insights

Data flows everywhere in the organization. But, consuming and communicating the data insights is no easy task. Once your company starts collecting and combining all kinds of data, the next step which can be elusive is extracting value from it. Your data can hold incredible amounts of potential value, but not an ounce of any value can be generated unless insights are uncovered and translated into business outcomes or actions.

These days, you can use a variety of new tools to communicate the results of your analytics. Obviously, the choice of your communication tool will depend on the situation and your audience. It is a fact that visual analytics—also called data visualization—has dramatically advanced communication of data insights. Below are some of the typical visual analytics:

- Bar graphs
- Pie charts
- Line charts
- Scatter graphs

Ideally, the use of bar graphs, pie charts, line charts and scatter graphs can only scratch the surface of whatever you want to do with the visual display. More advanced visual display tools such as matrix plots, heat maps, bubble charts, and treemaps can provide more options for displaying the data insights.

With several data visualization tools, it can be challenging at some point to settle a particular method. In such a case, you can employ more advanced customized tools such as SAS Visual Analytics, Games and Gapminder to help you communicate your data insights effectively.

# Chapter 2: Basics of Data Analytics

Data analytics is a diverse subject matter. In part, this is because data analytics represent a broad range of disciplines, including (but not limited to) statistics, computer science and even communication. Furthermore, within each discipline, data analytics can use some different methodologies such as Quantitative and Qualitative Approaches to undertaking analytics.

Despite this diversity in methodologies, data analytics share some common characteristics. In this chapter, we delve deeper to provide you with a complete big picture view of data analytic basics. Are you ready?

# Planning a study

Just like any research process, proper planning is required for an effective data analytics process. The concrete steps that you'll follow during the planning phase will depend, in part, on the problem to be investigated in the organization, availability of data analytic tools and a host of other factors. Nonetheless, it is precise to say that much of data analytics will follow the systematic course of actions.

Below are questions that you should ask yourself at the planning stage:

- What is the problem that needs to be investigated in the organization?
- How will data be collected?
- Which are data analytic tools available for data analysis?

Answering the above questions will provide you with a roadmap for your data analytic process. Next up, you should proceed to the data collection stage.

# Surveys

Flawed data can guide even the greatest data analytics in the wrong directions. You should be absolutely sure that you're getting the accurate data using the right methods. Surveys can have a significant impact on the direction of your company when it comes to data analytics. Before creating your survey, it's vital to think about its objective. The common goals of most surveys include:

- Compiling the market research in your organization
- Soliciting feedback from your customers
- Monitoring the performance of your organization

For you to design a proper survey, you should note down the specific knowledge that you'd like to gain from the survey along with the problems that you had identified during the planning stage.

Next up, identify the answers to the questions that you'd like to answer and write down the percentage of the responses that you would like to get from the data analytics. Comparing the future results against your expectation will provide the best guess on how you'll proceed with data analysis.

The pre-survey process will also help you to synthesize the important aspects of the survey process and guide you through the design process. Always remember that the larger scope the survey will reduce the number of respondents that can take participate in the survey.

Also, the manner in which you structure your questions and answers will help define the limits of the analysis when you summarize the results. The four primary response data types should guide you when structuring your questions:

- Categorical data. These include unordered labels such as colors or brand names. This is the simplest type of data that can help you analyze data because you'll only be limited to calculating the share of the responses in each category.
- Ordinal. These will provide you with a Likert scale with labels such as "Strongly Disagree" and "Strongly Agree."
- Interval. It will help you structured questions that include ranges such as "Number of employees."
- Ratio. It will help you structure issues such as "Inches of rain."

## Experiments

The experimental data is generated from a measurement, test method or experimental design. For instance, you can use an experimental design to produce results in clinical trials experiment. Experimental data can either be qualitative or quantitative with each discipline focusing on different investigations.

In an experiment, you'll attempt to observe the results of the experiment conducted intentionally so that you discover useful insights from it or demonstrate a known fact. With an experiment, you'll be able to draw conclusions concerning that factor of the study group as you make inferences from a sample to the larger population of interest. When designed correctly, an experiment can help you establish a cause-and-effect relationship between different variables.

## Gathering Data

Gathering data is the process of collecting and measuring information on the targeted variables based on established systematic fashion that allows you to answer basic questions about your analytic process. Ms Excel is familiar and easy-to-use software that can help you collect and manipulate data. When using Excel to gather data, you should know how to use the tables.

This process begins by setting up an appropriate data preparation.

During data preparation, the rule of thumb in using Excel is setting up the data table.

# Setting up the Excel table

Organizing Ms Excel data table can save you lots of time during data analytics. Basically, Ms Excel table is arranged in rows and columns. Each row represents one chunk of data. In RDBMSs terminologies, this is what forms one record. Depending on the nature of your Excel table, a record can be the customer's contact information or the invoice data.

Columns hold one type of data for each record. In RDBMSs terminologies, this is what forms one field. For instance, if your Ms Excel table contains data about customers, then one field can be the customer name while another one can be the customer address of the customer and so on. The first row of the Excel table should usually is reserved for the column headers. It is at the row headers that you will place field names such as "Customer Name" and "Customer Address". Ms Excel uses these names as the labels for the data entry form.

*Here are tips for effective Ms Excel data structure:*

- All the data should be entered in a single spreadsheet file.
- Always enter variable names in the first row of the spreadsheet file.
- The variable names should not be longer than eight characters and should start with a letter.
- The variable names should not contain spaces. However, they can start with an underscore character.
- There should be no other text rows such as the titles in the spreadsheet.
- There should be no blank rows appearing in the Excel data.
- If you have multiple groups of data, place them in the same spreadsheet together with variable names that show group membership.
- Avoid using the alphabetic characters for values.

- If your data group has two levels such as Male or Female, coding them using 0 and 1 makes sense as it allows easier analysis.
- For missing data values, always leave the cell blank.
- It is a good practice to enter dates using the slashes such as 5/05/2017) and the times with colons such as (12:15 AM).

However, keying data into the worksheet and moving the cursor after each and every entry can be frustrating. Fortunately, Ms Excel has data entry forms that can ease your pain. With only a sprint of the setup and knowledge of forms, Ms Excel can fast-track the process of data collection when you use the forms. After setting up your Ms Excel table, you should now proceed to set up Ms Excel form that will help you to capture the data.

## Setting up the Excel Form

The following are steps that will help you configure an Excel data form:

- Highlight the entire data and click on the Home ribbon.
- While on the Home ribbon, Click on Table, and select any one of the table styles that you see. With this done, you're now ready to set up your form.
- Now ensure you have displayed the Forms Button. If you're using Excel 2007, the Forms Button will not be available. For you to view it use the Quick Access Menu to add it or follow the following steps:
    a) Right-click any empty space on the Excel ribbon and select "Customize the Ribbon."
    b) In the dialog box that shows up, set "Choose commands from:" to choose Commands that are not in the Ribbon.
    c) On the right-hand of the Excel Window, select Data and click on the "New Group" button.

d) On the left-hand side of the Window, click "Form…"

e) Finally, with both the "Form…" and New Group (Custom) highlighted, click the Add >> button.

With this done, you can now set up your form.

- The headers that you will have specified in the top row of the Excel table will now be the field names. By default, the dialog box that crops us when you fire the Form Wizard shows the first existing record that you had entered in your table. You can browse and change the current records as you wish with the "Find Next" and "Find Prep" buttons.

- To add another record or row to Excel table, just click the "New" button. When you're done, click the "Close" button. This way, you'll find the process of data entry using Excel much simpler than you thought.

## Selecting a useful sample

The process of data analysis begins with identifying the population from which you'll obtain data. Because it's practically impossible to get data on every subject in the population, you should use an appropriate sampling technique to get a sample size that's representative. A typical statistical process is a four-step phase activity that includes the following:

- Estimate the expected proportion of the population that you want to study. The proportion of that population must of interest to the study.

- Determine the confidence interval for use in your analysis. Think of confidence level as the "margin of error" in your sample size. Now, all the empirical estimates are based on a sample that must have a certain degree of uncertainty. It's a must for you to specify the desired total spectrum of the confidence interval.

- Set the value of the confidence level. This provides the precision or level of uncertainty in the analysis. A narrow confidence interval that has a high confidence level such as 99% is likely to be as representative of the population as possible.

- Determine the sample size. Samples are often too large. This can waste time, resources and money using them as the basis for data analytics. On the other hand, when the sample size is too small, it can lead to inaccurate results. If you know the confidence level and the population size, you can use a statistical table to estimate your sample size. If the number that is required is too large, you can recalculate it with lower confidence levels or use wider intervals to choose a smaller sample size.

---

## Avoiding bias in a data set

Bias in any data set is a mortal enemy of both experimental and survey research. Therefore, it's important to guard against any biases that may arise in a data set. Bias can occur during the planning, data collection, analytics, and even publication stages of the research. Understanding biases in data sets can allow you to critically and independently review all data analytic literature.

A thorough understanding of bias in datasets and how it impacts the analytic results is essential for the practice of evidence-based decision making in organizations. Bias in data sets can be categorized into the following groups:

- Pre-trial bias. The sources of the pre-trial bias include errors from the study design and in respondents' recruitment causing fatal flaws in the results of the analytics which can't be compensated during data analysis. These errors can be avoided by careful selection of the sample size and wording of the questions to be used in the analytics.

- Bias during data collection. These are errors that occur in measurements of any exposure or outcomes. For instance, the information obtained and recorded from respondents in different study groups may be different. To avoid such errors, the data collection instruments have to be cleaned to ensure they are valid and reliable.

- Bias during publication phase. Some errors may occur during the presentation of the study results. For instance, citation and confounding errors can happen at the publication stage of the analytics process. To curb these mistakes, the data must be tested for reliability and validity to ensure it conforms to the problem at hand.

# Explaining Data

We have so far explored an overview of data analytics and the central concepts behind data analytics. But even before we proceed, let's start off by answering the question: "What is data?"

Well, the word data conjures different meanings depending on the context in which it is used. In measurements or statistics, data can be viewed as factual information that forms the foundations of reasoning, discussion, and calculations. In a sense, we can use data to provide facts about the performance of an organization or the economic growth of a country.

In computer science, data refers to raw facts such as numbers, characters, images that can be captured by any method of recording. These raw facts are meaningless when presented to users. For them to be meaningful, they have to be processed into information. It is the information that helps firms to make decisions about some action.

The majority of people believe that data has no meaning until it's interpreted or processed to make it meaningful. Whenever we carefully examine data to find out patterns in it for significant decisions to be made, we're actually using it as a component that generates knowledge. In understanding what data entails, it's vital to know that it can be collected in any form. It could be in numbers, pictures, maps, words or even in newspaper articles.

I know you're asking: "Which data format is better?"

Well, all the formats are better depending on what you would like to analyze. Ideally, the type of data that you'll be dealing with will be either qualitative or quantitative.

### Qualitative data

Data is said to be qualitative if it can be described in words. In other words, whatever you observe in the data is what you'll record. The observation can be based on color observations, odor or even texture.

For instance, suppose you are a marine biologist studying the behavior and the activities of dolphins. Surely, you will be identifying different dolphins within the group and observing them on a frequent basis. If you are recording their detailed observations, then the following will form the qualitative data.

- The colors of dolphin range from gray to white.
- When placed in a pod, the dolphins engage in play behavior.
- Dolphins have smooth skins

## Quantitative data

The data that we say is quantitative must have numeric measurements. Ideally, such data must be objective. By objective, I mean that the data must be the same regardless of who measures it. For instance, in qualitative data, different people can observe different colors for the same dolphin if one is a color blind.

However, in quantitative data, it must be the same. For instance, measurements such as length, mass, temperature, time, concentration and frequency will always be objective. Going back to our earlier example of research on dolphin, the following are examples of quantitative data that you can collect:

- There are thirteen dolphins in the pod.
- Dolphins eat an equivalent of 10-12% of their body mass each day.
- The sonar frequency that dolphins use is approximately 100 kHz.

Now that you understand what data entails let's examine the importance of data analytics to businesses.

# Descriptive Analytics

Statistics can be grouped into two broad categories namely descriptive and inferential statistics. The primary function of descriptive analytics is to summarize the data based on what has happened in the organization. It examines the raw data or content to provide answers to the following questions:

- What happened?
- What is happening?

In particular, descriptive analytics provides brief and summarized descriptively for a given data set, which can be a representational — if the sample size was used — or the entire population if the census method was used to study the population. Think of descriptive statistics as that branch of statistics which analyzes a big chunk of data to provide summarized charts using descriptive measures such as:

- The measures of central tendency such as mean, mode, and median.
- The measures of dispersion such as range, variance, and standard deviation.
- The measures of a shape such as skewness.

Descriptive analytics are usually broken down into measures of the central tendency and measures of the variability. When you use descriptive analytics to summarize your data, the following data visualization tools can help you communicate the results:

- Bar graphs
- Pie charts

- Line charts
- Scatter graphs
- Bubble graphs
- Treemaps

# Chapter 3: Descriptive Statistics

Descriptive statistics is a branch of statistics that provides brief and summarized descriptively for a given data set, which can be a representational—if the sample size was used—or the entire population if the census method was used to study the population. It is usually grouped into two broad categories:

- Measures of central tendency
- Measures of dispersion

## Measures of central tendency

These measures tries to describe a data set by identifying the core position within that data set. Intrinsically, measures of central tendency—which are sometimes called measures of central location—provides a single score that best describes the entire data distribution.

The common examples of measures of central tendency are:

- The mean
- The mode
- The median

In this chapter, we explore the measures of central tendency to provide you with an understanding of how to use each of them. Let's dive in.

## The mean

The mean—or the average— is the most popular and well-known measure of central tendency. The mean can be used with both discrete and continuous data. The mean is equivalent to the sum of all values in the data set divided by number of values in the data set. For instance, if you're given n values in a data set of $X_1$, $X_2$,...$X_n$, then the mean can be given as:

$$\bar{x} = \frac{(x_1 + x_2 + \cdots + x_n)}{n}$$

The above formula can also be re-written as:

$$\bar{x} = \frac{\sum x}{n}$$

The mean is, in essence, a model of your entire dataset. It is the value that is most common in most data distributions. It tries to minimize errors in the prediction of any one value that is present in your data set. By this I mean the value that produces the lowest amount of error from all the other values in the given data set.

However, the mean has one main flaw: it is susceptible to the influence of the outliers. In some datasets, there may be values that are unusual compared to the rest of the data set by either being too small or too large. Consider the table below:

| Staff | 1 | 2 | 3 | 4 | 5 | 6 | 7 | 8 | 9 | 10 |
|---|---|---|---|---|---|---|---|---|---|---|
| Salary | 15k | 18k | 16k | 14k | 15k | 15k | 12k | 17k | 90k | 95k |

The mean salary for the ten staff is $30.7k. Now, by inspecting the raw data set, you can realize that the mean value isn't the best way to accurately demonstrate the typical salary of any worker since the majority of workers has salaries in the range of $12k to 18k. Therefore, we can say the two large salaries have skewed the mean.

## The median

The median is the middle score for any data set which has been arranged in order of magnitude. Unlike mean, the median is less affected by the outliers and skewed data. Consider the table below:

| 65 | 55 | 89 | 56 | 35 | 14 | 56 | 55 | 87 | 45 | 92 |
|---|---|---|---|---|---|---|---|---|---|---|

To compute the median, we have to arrange the data set from smallest data value to the largest data value or vice versa. Here is what we get when we organize the data set from smallest value to the largest value:

| 14 | 35 | 45 | 55 | 55 | **56** | 56 | 65 | 87 | 89 | 92 |
|----|----|----|----|----|----|----|----|----|----|----|

Note that our table has 11 data elements. Therefore the middle value is the sixth term which can be obtained by the formula:

Median term= (n+1)/2

Is 56. 56 is the median value there are 5 scores before it and 5 other scores after it.

### The mode

It is the frequent score in any given dataset. If you're using a histogram, the mode will represent the highest bar in the bar chart or the histogram.

# Measures of Dispersion

The measures of dispersion—also called measures of variability, scatter, or the spread—are descriptive statistical measures that determine the extent to which a given data distribution is stretched or squeezed. The most common examples of measures of statistical dispersion are:

- The variance
- The standard deviation
- The coefficient of variation

This chapter explores the measures of dispersion to provide you with an understanding of how to use each of them. Let's dive in.

## The variance

The variance—which is abbreviated as $\sigma^2$—is a measure of how far each data value in the data set is from the mean. To calculate the $\sigma^2$ of a given data set, follow the procedures below:

- Compute the mean of the data set.
- Deduct the mean from each data value in the set. This provides you with a measure of the distance of each data value from the mean.
- Square each of these distances—to obtain all positive values—and sum all of the squares together.
- Divide the sum of the squares by the total number of values in the data set.

Mathematically, the variance of a given data set can be defined as:

$$\sigma^2 = \frac{\sum(X - \mu)^2}{N}$$

Note in the above formula that the variance is simply the sum of the squared distances of each data value in the distribution from the mean ($\mu$), divided by the total number of terms in the distribution (N).

As an example, consider the example below:

Let's go back to the two distributions that we started looked at in our first example.

Dataset 1: 3, 4, 4, 5, 6, 8

Dataset 2: 1, 2, 4, 5, 7, 11 .

Suppose we want to compute the variance of each data set, we'll first construct a table that calculates the values. Here is how the table will appear after taking into consideration all the terms in the formula for computing variance:

| Dataset | N | $\Sigma X$ | $\Sigma X^2$ | M | $\mu^2$ | $\sigma^2$ |
|---------|---|------------|--------------|---|---------|------------|
| 1 | 6 | 30 | 166 | 5 | 25 | 2.67 |
| 2 | 6 | 30 | 216 | 5 | 25 | 11 |

Even though both the data sets have the same mean ($\mu = 5$), the variance ($\sigma^2$) of the second data set is 11.00, which is a little more than four times the variance of the first data set at 2.67.

## The standard deviation

The standard deviation is the square root of the variance. Below are steps that you can follow when computing the standard deviation:

- Calculate the mean of the data set.
- Deduct the mean from each data value in the set. This provides you with a measure of the distance of each data value from the mean.
- Square each of these distances—to obtain all positive values—and sum all of the squares together.
- Divide the sum of the squares by the total number of values in the data set.

- Find the square root of the sum of the sum of squares divided by the total number of data values.

Mathematically, the standard deviation of a data set can be defined as follows:

$$\sigma = \sqrt{\frac{1}{N}\sum_{i=1}^{N}(x_i - \mu)^2}$$

Let's now use our previous example on variance to compute the variance. We have two data sets:

Dataset 1: 3, 4, 4, 5, 6, 8

Dataset 2: 1, 2, 4, 5, 7, 11 .

We'll proceed and construct the table as follows:

| Dataset | N | $\Sigma X$ | $\Sigma X^2$ | M | $\mu^2$ | $\sigma^2$ | $\sigma$ |
|---------|---|------------|--------------|---|---------|------------|----------|
| 1 | 6 | 30 | 166 | 5 | 25 | 2.67 | |
| 2 | 6 | 30 | 216 | 5 | 25 | 11 | |

Note that we have now added an extra column for standard deviation. To compute the values of $\sigma$, we'll simply get the square root of $\sigma$.

Here's how the table appears after getting the square roots of the variance:

| Dataset | N | $\Sigma X$ | $\Sigma X^2$ | M | $\mu^2$ | $\sigma^2$ | $\sigma$ |
|---------|---|------------|--------------|---|---------|------------|----------|
| 1 | 6 | 30 | 166 | 5 | 25 | 2.67 | 1.63 |

| 2 | 6 | 30 | 216 | 5 | 25 | 11 | 3.32 |
|---|---|----|-----|---|----|----|------|

## Coefficients of Variation

The Coefficient of Variation (CV) defines the amount of variability relative to the mean. Since the CV is unit-less, you can use it instead of the standard deviation when you want to compare the spread of data sets that have different units or even various means.

For instance, you are the quality control examiner at milk bottle manufacturing plant that bottles small and large containers. You take a sample of each milk product and observe that the mean volume of the smaller containers is 1 cup with a standard deviation of 0.08. You also find out that the average volume of the large containers is 1 gallon or 16 with a standard deviation of 0.4.

You can note that the standard deviation of the gallon container is nearly five times greater that of the smaller containers. However, when you compute their CVs, you'll find out a different measure. For instance, the CVs is:

| Larger container | Smaller container |
|------------------|-------------------|
| CV = 100 * 0.4 cups / 16 cups = 2.5 | CV = 100 * 0.08 cups / 1 cup = 8 |

The CV of the small container (8) is more than three times greater than the CV of the large container (2.5). In other words, even though the large container has a higher standard deviation, the smaller bottle has more variability relative to its mean.

## Drawing conclusions

Both variance and standard deviation provide a numerical measure of scattering for a given data set. These measures are helpful when making comparisons between data sets that go beyond the simple visual impressions. The standard deviation can be difficult to interpret if it is presented as a single number. However, a smaller value for standard deviation implies that the values in the dataset are close to the mean of the data set.

On the other hand, a large standard deviation suggests that the values in the statistics set are farther away from the mean. A smaller value for the standard deviation can be a goal in certain scenarios where the results are restricted, for instance, in the product manufacturing and quality control systems. A particular type of vehicle part that has to be 3 centimeters in diameter to fit properly had better not have a large standard deviation during the construction process.

On the other hand, a large standard deviation in such a scenario would imply that lots of vehicle parts will end up in the trash since they don't fit properly. But in scenarios where you just observe and record statistical data, a large standard deviation may not necessarily be a bad thing since it just shows a large amount of variation in the group of elements that are being studied.

For instance, when you look at salaries for every employee of a certain company ranging from the student intern to the CEO, you may find that the standard deviation may be large. When you narrow down the group by examining only the student interns, you'll find out that the standard deviation is smaller. This is because the individuals within such a group will always have salaries that are less variable.

# Chapter 4: Charts and Graphs

Ms Excel provides an excellent range of great charts that can help visualize your data. You can exploit these full ranges of visualization tools to help you explore your data and create reports that have color-coded data values with interactive slicers. The following guidelines should be considered when visualizing data in Ms Excel:

- Always use the Power View when exploring data with a range of data visualizations. The Power View is vital when you want to establish relationships between data that exists in multiple tables.
- You can use the Power Map to show the changes in geographically-related dispersed data values over a given time.
- Use the native Pivot Charts and the conditional formatting when creating data visualizations in workbooks that will be launched in versions of Excel that don't support Power View or the Power Map.

Below are common tools that you can use to visualize the data:

- Pie charts
- Bar graphs
- Time charts
- Line graphs
- Histograms
- Scatter plots

Let's jump in to explore how these data visualization tools can help you during analytics.

# #1: Pie charts

For you want to visualize data in the form of slices to the total value or pie, then you should consider using pie charts. Pie charts usually display the contribution of each value—or the slice—to a total (pie). Pie charts rely on one data series. Here is an example of a pie chart:

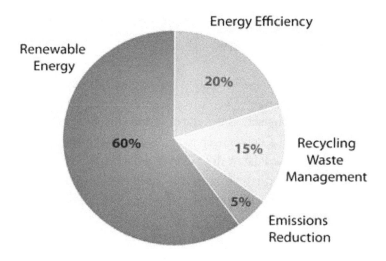

Here are steps that you should follow if you want to create a pie chart in Ms Excel:

**Step One:** Type your data into the Microsoft Excel worksheet. You can begin by typing your categories in one column and the numbers in a second column. Don't leave blank rows or columns when typing data in the Excel sheet.

**Step two:** Highlight the data you've just entered. To highlight the data, click on the top left of your data and then drag the mouse cursor to the bottom right.

*Step three*: Click on "Insert," followed by "Pie," and then click the type of pie chart you want from the menu that appears. If you want a simple pie chart such as the one shown above, a 2D selection will work fine. Once you have clicked on the chart icon, Ms Excel will automatically insert the pie chart into your worksheet.

If you made a mistake your data entries, you don't have to start afresh. Just type your correction in the original data and Ms Excel will automatically update the pie chart.

## #2: Bar graphs

Bar graphs can be used to display data in the form of horizontal or vertical rectangular bars. The bars levels off the appropriate level to define values on the plane. Below is an example of a bar chart:

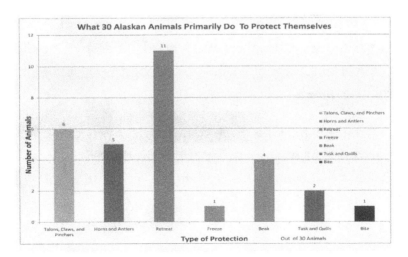

Here are quick steps that can help you create a bar graph in Ms Excel:

*Step One:* Type your data into the Microsoft Excel worksheet. You can begin by typing your categories in one column and the numbers in a second column. Don't leave blank rows or columns when typing data in the Excel sheet.

*Step two:* Highlight the data you've just entered. To highlight the data, click on the top left of your data and then drag the mouse cursor to the bottom right.

*Step three*: Click on "Insert," followed by "Bar," and then click the type of pie chart you want from the menu that appears. If you want a simple pie chart such as the one shown above, a 2D selection will work fine. Once you have clicked on the chart icon, Ms Excel will automatically insert the pie chart into your worksheet.

*Step Four*: Switch the axes, if necessary by clicking on "Axes" on the Ribbon and typing the labels for axes.

*Step five*: Adjust your labels and legends, if desired by clicking on "Labels and Legends" on the Ribbon and typing in the appropriate labels.

If you made a mistake your data entries, you don't have to start afresh. Just type your correction in the original data and Ms Excel will automatically update the pie chart.

# #3: Time charts

A time series chart—also called times series graph—is an illustration of the data points at successive time intervals. A time chart can help evaluate patterns and behavior in data over a given time. It usually displays the observations on the y-axis against the equally spaced time intervals on the x-axis. Here's an example:

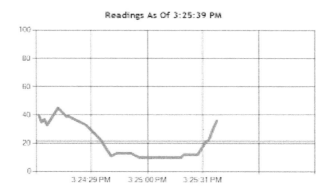

## #4: Line Graphs

The line graphs are used to compare changes that take place over the same period for more than one group of data. Here is an example of a line graph:

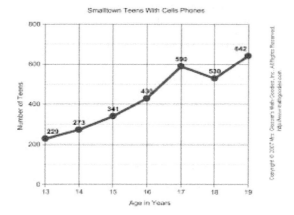

Here are quick steps that you should follow if you want to create a line chart in Ms Excel:

*Step One:* Type your data into the Microsoft Excel worksheet. You can begin by typing your categories in one column and the numbers in a second column. Don't leave blank rows or columns when typing data in the Excel sheet.

*Step two:* Highlight the data you've just entered. To highlight the data, click on the top left of your data and then drag the mouse cursor to the bottom right.

*Step three*: Click on "Insert," followed by "Line," and then click the type of line chart you want from the menu that appears.

If you made a mistake your data entries or you want to insert another set of data you don't have to start afresh. Just type your correction in the original data or add the extra data in the rows and columns you had created, and Ms Excel will automatically update the pie chart.

---

# #5: Histograms

A histogram—also called a frequency polygon—is a graph formed by joining of the midpoints of histogram column tops. The histograms are used when depicting data from the continuous variables. Below is an example of a histogram:

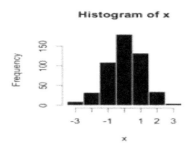

Here are steps to follow when creating a histogram in Ms Excel:

*Step one*: Load the Data Analysis Toolpak, if it hasn't been installed. To confirm if the Toolpak is installed, click on the "Data" tab and check the far right. When you see Data Analysis, then the Toolpak is installed. If it hasn't been installed, click on "File" followed by "Option." In the menu that appears, click on "Analysis Toolpak" and follow the onscreen instructions to install it.

*Step two*: Enter the data into a single column of your Excel sheet. For instance, type your values into column A.

*Step three*: Enter your BINs (Boundary intervals) into a single column (for example, column B) For example, if you have data sets 0-10, 11-20 and 21-30 you can enter 10, 20, 30 in column B.

*Step Four*: Click the *"Data"* tab and then click the *"Data Analysis"* button.

*Step five*: Select *"Histogram"* and then click the "**OK**" button.

*Step six*: Type the location of your data in Input Range Box that appears. For instance, if your data is in cells A3 to A13 then type A3: A13 into the box.

*Step Seven*: Type the location of the BINS into the *"Bin Range"* input box. For example, type "B3: B13" into the input box to indicate your BINS are in cells B3 to B13.

*Step Eight*: Select the option the location of your histogram.

*Step Nine*: Check the "**Chart Output**" input box. If you don't check this, you will only get a frequency chart and not the actual histogram.

*Step ten*: Click on the "OK" button, and Ms Excel will create the histogram.

## #6: Scatter plots

The scatter plots are similar to the line graphs because they also use the horizontal and vertical axes to plot data points. However, scatterplots have a very specific purpose — to show how much one variable is affected or is related to another or correlation. Here is an example of a scatter plot:

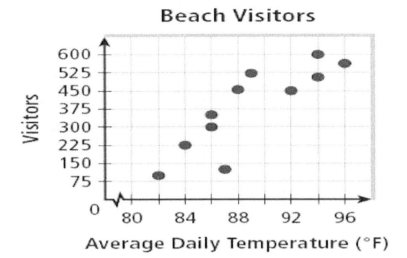

**Beach Visitors**

Visitors (y-axis): 600, 525, 450, 375, 300, 225, 150, 75

Average Daily Temperature (°F) (x-axis): 80, 84, 88, 92, 96

Here are quick steps for creating scatterplots in Ms Excel:

*Step One:* Type your data into the Microsoft Excel worksheet. You can begin by typing your categories in one column and the numbers in a second column. Don't leave blank rows or columns when typing data in the Excel sheet.

*Step two:* Highlight the data you've just entered.

*Step three*: Click on "Insert," followed by "Scatter," and then click the type of scatter chart you want from the menu that appears. If you want a simple pie chart such as the one shown above, a 2D selection will work fine. Once you have clicked on the chart icon, Ms Excel will automatically insert the scatterplot into your worksheet.

If you made a mistake your data entries, you don't have to start afresh. Just type your correction in the original data and Ms Excel will automatically update the pie chart.

# Chapter 5: Application of Data Analytics to Business and Industry

The bottom line of any data analytic process is unearthing the "hidden" value in data sets. In particular, data Analytics applies both statistical and logical techniques to describe, condense and evaluate raw data with the goal of unraveling insightful information that can aid in decision making. This chapter explores the applications of data analytics to businesses and the industry.

## Business Intelligence

Business intelligence (BI) combines data warehousing, predictive business analytics, business strategies, performance and user interface to help organizations attain a strategic competitive advantage. The BI applications receive data from the internal and external environment and organize it into a form suitable for utilization in the organization.

Here are some applications of BI in organizations:

- Banking. BI systems are used in banks to predict the customers' ability to be advanced loans. The BI applications can determine whether a customer's credit rating is "good" or "bad" based on parameters such as age, current savings, and income.
- Supply chain management. When applied in supply chain and management, BI can scale up internal efficiencies to allow organizations use their operational data for trend analysis and craft better business strategies to achieve profitability.
- Manufacturing. The BI software can sift through large sets data from across the supply chain and provide insightful information to the company for better decisions about managing inventories.
- Public sector. BI can help governments design fraud detection systems and personnel attrition.
- Healthcare. BI is a must-implement solution for healthcare providers that want to standardize data, reduce healthcare data redundancy and costs while complying with industry standards for enhanced efficiencies.
- Customer Relationship Management. BI platforms can consolidate data into a central place to allow organizations improve and expand their existing relationships about improving customer service using historical data on all the previous customer interactions.

# Data analytics in business and industry

Across all the industries, big data and advanced analytics are helping businesses to become smarter and better at making predictions that are improving productivity. Today, most companies have recognized that they have opportunities to use big data and analytics to raise their productivity, improve decision making, and gain a strategic competitive advantage. Here are reasons why data analytics has become a buzzword in the majority of organizations:

- Data analytics provides large statistical samples that enhance analytic tool results. The majority of tools that are designed for data mining tend to be optimized for large data sets providing firms with the abilities to deal with large sets of data.
- Analytic tools and databases can now handle big data by executing large queries and parse tables in record time. The recent generations of vendor-specific tools and platforms have increased the rate information flow in organizations allowing them to make prompt decisions.
- Big data is a is vital  in leveraging with analytics. The new technologies and best practices have improved processing capabilities allowing organizations to harness archive data to helpful insights.

# Chapter 6: Final Thoughts on Data Analytics

Although we've focused on beginner topics for data analytics, there are still a lot of valuable tools that have emerged in recent times. Besides Ms Excel, you should try to learn at least one the following data analytic programming languages if you want to take your professional career to the next level:

- Python
- R
- MatLab
- Julia
- Hadoop
- Perl
- Julia

Strictly speaking, no language will fit all the analytic data problems. Each language has its own strengths and weaknesses. If you are an experienced programmer, I will advise you to start off with Python or R.

Besides learning these languages, it's important for me to mention that technology is changing fast. And really fast! Therefore, as a data scientist, there will always be some disruptive technologies coming on board to destabilize the conventional systems that you're familiar with. If there's one thing that's fuelling the rise of these disruptive technologies, then it is big data.

In the recent past, organizations have been dealing with structured data which can easily be organized into tables and analyzed using the conventional RDBMSs. But today, firms are processing massive amounts of data that are either semi-structured or unstructured. To make matters worse, this data has a high velocity meaning that computational power has to increase.

At this rate, the conventional systems that you may be used to aren't sufficient.

In recent times, smart contracts have emerged as the future technology of analytics.

Smart contracts are program codes that can facilitate, execute, and enforce negotiations or performance agreements—Contract—using the Blockchain technology. These codes can act as substitutes for legal contracts where the terms of the contracts encoded in a computer programming language as a set of instructions.

The potential to link smart contracts to data analytics is perhaps one of the first steps towards creating a new world of opportunities. Now with advances in IoT that connect to cloud computing, wireless sensors and physical objectives that include small computer chips, smart contracts can provide these inanimate objects the level of artificial intelligence for data analytics in the 21st century.

But the use of smart contracts in these areas is yet to be seen. How the enforcement of smart contracts in code form and the prevailing laws and regulations in practice is still the greatest challenge that has to be resolved to realize the real potentials of smart contracts in data analytics.

# Conclusion

Companies have had serious difficulties in harnessing their data into meaningful insights in the last couple of years. Because of skyrocketing volumes of data, today's interest in data analytics is unparalleled. While previous analysis centered on a few specific departments, today's analysis has to focus on all the departments of the organization.

Data analytics provides the only hope for fact-based, and insightful-driven decisions can help organizations manage their strategic, operation and financial performance that can help them increase their shareholder value. That's why it's no longer tenable to ignore data analytics.

I hope that you've grasped all the basics of data analytics that you were looking out for in this book.

**If you found this book useful, please take a moment to leave a review on Amazon as it'd greatly help us to improve our future ebooks for great customers like yourself!**

# Further Reading

Below are websites that can help you explore more about data analytics

1. **https://www.sas.com**
2. **https://halobi.com/2016/07/descriptive-predictive-and-prescriptive-analytics-explained/**
3. **http://www.kdnuggets.com/2014/06/top-10-data-analysis-tools-business.html**
4. **http://www.informationbuilders.com/data-analysis**
5. **https://ori.hhs.gov/education/products/n_illinois_u/datamanagement/datopic.html**
6. **http://www.bigskyassociates.com/blog/bid/356764/5-Most-Important-Methods-For-Statistical-Data-Analysis**
7. **http://www.thearling.com/text/dmwhite/dmwhite.htm**
8. **http://www.makeuseof.com/tag/create-free-survey-collect-data-excel/**
9. **https://oit.utk.edu/research/documentation/Documents/HowToUseExcelForDataEntry.pdf**
10. **https://www.skillsyouneed.com/num/statistics-identifying-patterns.html**
11. **http://homepages.rpi.edu/~bennek/class/mmld/talks/lecture2-05.ppt**

# Markov Models

**Understanding Data Science, Markov Models And Unsupervised Machine Learning In Python**

## TECHWORLD

# At a glance

By allowing computers to perform explicit tasks intelligently, today's machine learning systems can carry out multifaceted processes by learning from data, instead of following pre-programmed instructions. Recent years have seen stirring developments in machine learning, making it useful in a horde of applications.

While mounting data availability has enabled machine learning systems to be trained on a vast pool of samples, increasing computing capabilities in modern computers has also propelled the analytical potentials of these systems. Within the field of machine learning itself, there have been algorithmic advances that have given it a greater power.

One such advancement is in the unsupervised machine learning algorithms arena. By their very nature, unsupervised machine learning algorithms cluster a given population in different groups making them suitable for segmenting customers into the various groups for particular intervention measures. As a result, computer systems which only a few years ago performed strikingly below human levels are now outperforming human beings in some tasks.

Clearly, the primary aim of machine learning is to train the computers or machine to learn on its own and make informed decisions in a relatively short time than what human beings can do. While the promising applications of machine learning grow daily, the time and effort required to train such optimized machine learning systems are substantial. Constant training and providing information isn't the natural way for these machines to learn and obtain the necessary knowledge.

All these factors point to the treasured potentials of unsupervised machine learning algorithms, which if done correctly can learn and deduct largely without human intervention. Today, you're likely to interact with all sorts of computer systems based on machine learning. From image recognition systems used on social media platforms to voice recognition systems used in personal assistants, the list of unsupervised machine learning keeps on expanding.

As the field grows further, the potentials of unsupervised machine learning will be revolutionary in both social and economic arenas. One type of unsupervised machine learning algorithm that continues to grow are Markov models. Markov models today are providing support for complex problems that involves uncertainties in a continuous period. With the ever-increasing computing power, Markov models are likely to play an active role in the growth of machine learning applications.

The primary objective of this book is to provide you with all the ins and outs of Markov models and unsupervised machine learning over a range of multi-faceted applications. Specifically, the book will explore practical implementations of Markov models in Python programming environment.

Are you ready?

Let's dive in!

# CONTENTS

# Chapter 1: Can Computers Learn Unsupervised?

In 2012, AI researchers from Google X lab and Stanford connected 1000 computers and turned them loose on 10 million YouTube images for three days. During this period, they kept on watching the computers to find out if the computers could identify the cat faces. And the results were interesting: they were all able to identify the cat faces on their own.

While perhaps this isn't what Turing had in mind when he coined the term Artificial Intelligence, it provides background insight upon which machines can learn on their own as opposed to using pre-determined instructions that we are used to in conventional programs. But what's most striking about the study is that the AI researchers didn't actually program the computers to identify the cat faces. The computers started doing that on their own.

Obviously, the ultimate goal of any machine learning system is to train the computer of the machine to learn and infer like a human being, while taking in much more data and making better choices in exponentially less time than human beings do. There are three types of machine learning: supervised learning, unsupervised learning and reinforcement learning.

In this chapter, we provide a background of these machine learning algorithms. Specifically, we'll dive deeper into unsupervised learning algorithms to provide you with a big picture view of Markov models.

# Types of machine learning algorithms

Obviously, learning is a broad domain. Therefore, the machine-learning field has several subfields that deal with different kinds of learning processes. Machine learning can be viewed from many different angles, depending on the learning process and its objectives. At the outset, machine learning can be grouped into three categories based on their goals:

- Supervised learning
- Unsupervised learning
- Reinforcement learning

Let's jump in to explore these types of machine learning.

## #1: Supervised learning

Supervised learning is the kind of learning that takes place when an algorithm learns from input data, and its associated target responds to predict future responses with new examples correctly. The associate's target responses can range from numerical values to string labels such as tags. Supervised learning resembles the human learning experience under the supervision of the teacher. When the teacher provides satisfactory examples to pupils in class, students memorize these examples and form conclusions from them.

Examples of these learning algorithms are:

- Decision Trees
- Random Forest
- KNN
- Regression Algorithms

## #2: Unsupervised learning

As the name suggests, unsupervised learning takes place when the program learns from the examples without associating it to any responses. In other words, the programmer leaves the algorithm to determine its own data patterns from the set of inputs it has. This type of algorithm usually restructures the data into new features that can represent a class or even a new series of uncorrelated values.

Unsupervised learning is quite useful in providing human beings with new insights into large sets of data and new inputs to the supervised machine learning algorithms. It resembles the approaches that people use to understand whether certain objects or events belong to the same class by using a degree of similarity.

Examples of unsupervised learning algorithms are:
- Clustering algorithms
- Neural Networks
- Markov algorithms


## #3: Reinforcement learning

Reinforcement learning is the type of learning that takes place when you provide the algorithm with inputs that lack labels, as in unsupervised learning. But for learning to take place, you must accompany the input with positive or negative feedback mechanisms depending on how the algorithm works. This type of learning is useful for applications that require the algorithm to make its own decisions.

In other words, the product must be prescriptive and not descriptive as is used in unsupervised learning. In human beings, we can regard reinforcement learning as learning by "trial and error." The errors help the program to understand its actions because they have penalties associated with them such as cost, time lost and so on.

This type of learning lets the algorithm to know the outcome of actions it will take where learning occurs while trying to avoid the mistakes. A perfect example of an application that uses reinforcement learning is the Google's DeepMind program that plays Atari games.

## Unsupervised Learning: the big picture

In supervised learning, the output is already determined. For instance, when a student is learning from an instructor, the outcome can always be pre-determined. All you need to do is work out the process to map the input to your output. If the algorithm comes up with results that are widely different from the training data, then the instructor steps in to guide the student back to the right track.

Unsupervised learning algorithms—where a lot of excitement over the future of AI stems—are more complex compared to supervised learning algorithms. In particular, there is no training data, and the outputs are unknown. Essentially, the computer goes into the problem blind with only its perfect logical operations to direct it.

Staggering as this may seem, unsupervised machine learning can solve multi-faceted problems with just the input data, and the logic mechanisms that are all computer systems are built on.

But how exactly does unsupervised learning work?

Let me use a basic example to illustrate how unsupervised learning can work.

Let's say we are having a digital image showing some colored geometric shapes. Now, we want to match these shapes into groups according to their classification and color. This is an image recognition problem that is a common problem in machine learning.

With supervised learning, the process is simple. All we have to do is teach the machine that any shape with four faces is a square while one with eight faces is an octagon. We can also learn the system that if the image has a light with certain values, then it is red, blue or green.

However, with unsupervised learning, the process is much different. We'll have the same input data, which is the geometrical shapes and the colors. The system will then use whatever logic is at its disposal to match the various shapes and their corresponding colors. Perhaps geometrical shapes with the same number of sides or those with matching digital markers can indicate the color.

Ideally, the AI agent knows for a certain that a particular object is a square or an octagon. But it will recognize other objects with approximately similar characteristics, group them together and assign its own label to the objects with a certain degree of probability for the same shapes. Technically speaking, there is no right or wrong outcome since there is no instructor to guide the learner. Because of this problem, the unsupervised learning algorithm can make mistakes. But just like human beings, the AI agent will learn from the errors and improve its estimations next time.

Some of the examples of unsupervised learning algorithms are Clustering Algorithm, Markov Algorithm, and the Neural Networks. Let's take some time to explore the clustering and the neural networks algorithms.

# Clustering Algorithm

The clustering algorithm is an unsupervised algorithm that solves the clustering problem. Its procedure follows a simple way to classify any given data set using a particular number of clusters (assume that k clusters). The data points inside a given cluster must be homogeneous and heterogeneous to the peer groups.

Can you figure out the shapes from the inkblots?

Well, the clustering algorithm is akin to this activity. In other words, you only look at the shape of the inkblot and decipher how many different clusters or population are present on that inkblot. In particular, here's how the algorithm will allow you to solve the learning problem:

The algorithm selects the k number of points for each of the clusters. For simplicity, these clusters will be called the centroids.

Each data point forms will now create the cluster with the closest centroids. In this case, we will have k clusters.

We now determine the centroid of each cluster based on the existing cluster members. This generates new centroids.

Since new centroids have been generated, step two and three are repeated to find out the closest distance for each data member from the generated centroids. The process is repeated until convergence occurs.

As we have new centroids, repeat step 2 and 3. Find the closest distance for each data point from new centroids and get associated with new k-clusters. Repeat this process until convergence occurs i.e. centroids does not change.

As we have seen, we will have clusters, and each cluster will have its centroid. The sum of the squares of differences between the centroid and the data points within the cluster will constitute the sum of square value for that cluster. Also, when the sum of the squared values for all the groups has been added, it will become total within the sum of square values for the cluster solution.

Below are some of the advantages of the Clustering Algorithm:

- It provides a higher computability when compared to other machine learning algorithms. For instance, when the variables are many the clustering algorithm can utilize fewer computer resources while offering the results that the learner wants.
- It provides tighter clusters that improve the efficiency of classification.

Some of the disadvantages of the Clustering Algorithm are:

- It is useful for classification problems. However, it may not work for prediction cases.
- If the first clusters are wrong, then the entire clustering may not produce the desired results.

## Neural Networks

Neural networks have different layers that can be used for analyzing and learning data. It is one of the most widely used algorithms for analyzing patterns. Every hidden layer will attempt to detect patterns on the picture that is being learned. If the pattern is detected the next hidden layer will be activated. That layer will again try to identify the model on the next picture.

Let me explain using an example.

Suppose you're dealing with the problem of recognizing the models of cars in your system. Then basically, the system must be made to learn the different patterns such as the color, the number plate and various features of the car for the Neural networks to learn and categorize. Suppose you bring your first car for detection.

Apparently, the first layer of the system will detect the edges of the car. Then the following layers will combine other others that have been found in car data. Ultimately, a specified layer will try to detect the wheel patterns or even the window profiles. Depending on the number of layers in your car, the system may or may not be able to specify what is in the picture. The more the layers of the neural network, the more the system will learn the patterns.

The Neural Networks learn and attribute the weights to the connections that exist between the different neurons every time the network processes data. This implies that the next time it comes across such a picture, it will have learned that this particular image is likely associated with a particular model of a car.

Below are some benefits of the Neural Networks:
- They require less formal statistical training
- They can implicitly detect complex nonlinear relationships between the dependent and independent variables.
- They can identify all the possible interactions between the predictor variables and the target variables.

Some of the disadvantages of the Neural Networks are:
- They require high computational power.
- They may not provide accurate relationships between the target variables and the predictor variables.

# Chapter 2: Introduction to Markov Models

This chapter explores the ins and outs of Markov models. Specifically, the section will provide a detailed account of the mathematics behind Markov models that makes them suitable for unsupervised machine learning. Before we start, let's define the term Markov model.

## What are Markov Models?

Markov models are stochastic processes that describe a sequence of possible events where the probability of each event depends only on the state that has been attained in the previous event. I know this definition may be confusing at this stage. Let me break it down for you.

Here in Kenya, we have three types of weather: sunny, rainy and foggy. Now, let us assume for a moment that the weather will last the entire day. In other words, the weather doesn't change from rainy to foggy in the middle of the day. Weather prediction is all about figuring how to guess what the weather will look like tomorrow based on the history of all observations of the weather.

Let's create a simplified model of weather prediction based on collected statistics. We'll gather all the information about what the weather was like today based on the information we gathered yesterday, the day before and so forth. Mathematically, we can represent this as follows:

$$P\left(w_n \mid w_n - 1, \; w_{n-2}, \ldots\ldots\ldots, \; w_1\right)$$

Using the above expression, we can now give probabilities of the types of weather for tomorrow and the next day using the $n$ days of history that we have collected. For instance, if we already know that the weather for the past three days has been sunny, sunny and foggy in that chronological order, then we'll have the following expression which models the probability that tomorrow will be rainy:

```
P (w₄=Rainy|w₃= Foggy, w₂= Sunny, w₁= Sunny)
```

While the above example may seem straightforward, the problem can become complicated when the size of n increases. In particular, the larger n is the more statistics value that we must collect for us to make predictions for data sets that are large. If n is 6, then we must collect $3^6$ statistics for these histories. The following Markov assumption can help us for any n data values:

```
P (wₙ|wₙ₋₁, wₙ₋₂, ............., w₁)
```

The above expression can be summarized as follows:

```
P (wₙ | wₙ₋₁)
```

The above expression forms the basis for Markov algorithms. We can interpret it as: the probability of an observation at any time n only depends on the observation at time n-1. Now that you know what Markov models are, how can they be applied in real-life situations?

Good question.

In practice, we never have access to any infinite number of observations. Therefore, the idea of the central limit theorem cannot apply when formulating learning problems for such cases. However, we can just use the approximation rule to apply to the real situation. Let me elaborate using the event of the dice.

Suppose throw up a dice, and you want to find its probability distributions in the event of the dice. In such then you want to state the worst-case bounds for the finite sums of the random variables to determine by how much the empirical expected mean is deviating from its expectation. Now, those bounds may not only be useful for the simple averages but also to help you to quantify the behavior of the more sophisticated estimators that are based on a set of observations.

The bounds that we've just discussed on the dice problem differ for knowledge they assume about the random variables in question. For example, when we want only to find only the mean of the distribution. It may be difficult to determine the mean because of the limitations of the models that we have discussed previously.

This leads us to the Markov Algorithm.

I know you're thinking, *"How does Markov Algorithm deal with the problem described above?"*

Well, Markov Algorithm is an example of an unsupervised learning algorithm (so the learner will have to figure out how himself how he will arrive at the solution). Suppose we know their mean and their variance then we will be in a position to state a stronger bound that can now help us determine the mean of the distribution.

For even more important settings, when we already know that each variable has bounded range, then we can apply the limits that can produce efficient output from the model. Ideally, the nature of the problem can help us determine the most probable set of parameters that dictates the input states based on the sequence of the output states.

Because of this property, Markov Algorithm has found its way in many learning problems where the data is already known but not the specific parameters for dictating the behavior. For instance, the sequencing of DNA can be modeled using the Markov Algorithm.

# The mathematics behind Markov algorithms

Machine learning is a broad field that intersects several disciplines such as statistics and probability theory and computer science. A thorough understanding of statistics and probability behind Markov models is necessary for a good grasp of developing intelligent systems. Here is a brief overview of probability theory concepts that will help you understand Markov models:

## #1: Probability axioms

Given any finite sample space $S$ and an event $A$ in the sample space $S$. We can define $P(A)$ as the probability of $A$ with the following assumptions:

$0 \leq P(A) \leq 1$ For each event A in S.

$P(S) = 1$

$P(A+B) = P(A) + P(B)$ only if $A$ and $B$ are mutually exclusive events in the sample space S.

## #2: Joint Probability

Suppose that $A$ and $B$ are random variables, then the joint probability function of $A$ and $B$ is $P(a,b) = P(A=a, B=b)$

# #3: Conditional Distributions

Conditional distributions provide one of the essential tools in probability theory that can help model systems that can reason about uncertainty. Conditional distributions define the distribution of the random variable when the value of another random variable is known. In other words, when some event is already known to be true, then we can determine the outcome of another event using conditional probability distributions.

Formally, the conditional probability of X = a given Y = b can be defined as

```
P(X = a|Y = b)  =  P(X = a, Y = b)/ P(Y = b)
```

Consider the following example.

Suppose we already know that the dice throw was odd, and want to determine the probability that a "one" has been thrown. Let X be the random variable of dice thrown, and Y be the indicator variable that assumes the value of 1 in case the thrown dice turns up odd. We can define our desired probabilities as:

```
P(X = 1|Y = 1)  =  P(X = 1, Y = 1)  P(Y = 1)  =  (1/6
)/(1/2)  = 1/3
```

# #4: Independence

Independence means that the distribution of the random variable doesn't change on learning of the value of another random variable. In machine learning, we can make assumptions about data based on independence. For instance, the training samples are assumed to be independent of some underlying space when the label of sample i is independent of the features of sample j (i 6= j).

Formally, a random variable X is independent of Y only when

```
P(X) = P(X|Y )
```

Note from the above example that we have now dropped what values the random variables X and Y are taking. This implies that the statement will hold true for any values that X and Y may take.

# #5: Product rule

From the definition of the conditional probability, the product rule can be defined as: $P(A,B) = P(A|B)P(B) = P(B|A)P(A)$

# #6: Chain rule

The chain rule is an extension of the product rule that can be summarized in more generic form as follows:

$$P(a_1, a_2, \ldots, a_n) = P(a_1 | a_2, \ldots, a_n) P(a_2 | a_3, \ldots, a_n) \ldots \ldots P(a_{n-1} | a_n) P(a_n)$$

# #7: Bayes' rule

Bayes' rule is an alternative method that helps to calculate the conditional probability if the joint probability of $P(A,B)$ is unknown. From the conditional probability, we already know that $P(A|B)P(B) = P(A,B)$ and $P(B|A)P(A) = P(A,B)$.

Bayes rule can be specified as:

$$P(A|B) = \frac{P(B|A)P(A)}{P(B)}$$

# Chapter 3: Markov Models and Unsupervised Learning

This chapter reviews an important concept of Markov models that is called the Markov property and its relationship to unsupervised learning. At the end of the chapter, you will have a big picture view of how Markov models can be applied in machine learning.

But we dive in let's start by exploring the Markov property.

## What is a Markov property?

A Markov property is derived from research done by a Russian scientist Andreevich Markov in 1913. Andreevich was studying the chain properties of both consonants and vowels in Russian literature in what is commonly called Pushkin's poems. He found out that both consonants and vowels formed a chain system where the present state and the past state have no influence on the future states.

This property is called the Markov property, and the systems that exhibit these characteristics are called Markov chains. In our previous chapter, we defined the conditional probability X = a given Y = b as:

```
P(X = a|Y = b) = P(X = a, Y = b)/ P(Y = b)
```

We also defined a Markov model as any system that exhibits the following properties:

```
P (Wₙ | Wₙ₋₁)
```

Based on the above definitions, the conditional probability that we can extend to Markov chains can be expressed as:

$$P(q_t|q_1, \cdots\cdots, q_{t-1}) = P(q_t|q_{t-1})$$

In the above expression, $q_t$ is the random variable of the Markov system at a given time $t$.

Next up, let's explore the Markov chains.

## Markov chains

Put simply, Markov chains are mathematical systems that change from one state—or a situation/set of values—to another. For instance, if you develop a Markov system for a baby's behavior, you can include "eating," "playing, "sleeping" and "crying" as the various states. These states, together with other behavior of the child is what forms the "state space"—a list of all the possible states in the Markov system.

Besides the state space, any Markov model should define the probability of hopping of transitioning from one state to another. For instance, the likelihood that the baby who is currently playing will fall asleep in the next ten minutes without crying.

In summary, a Markov chain is any system that has a state space and the probability distributions that define how the system should transition from one state to another. Within the state space, we have to define the observation sequence and the state sequence.

Now, the probability of the observed sequence, which is usually written as $P(y_1^T)$, can be computed by determining the joint probability of both the observation sequence and the state sequence $P(y_1^T, q_1^T)$.

The term $P(y_1^T, q_1^T)$ is recursively factored using the conditional probability and the chain rules. Therefore,

$$P(y_1^T, q_1^T) = P(y_T, q_T | y_1^{T-1}, q_1^{T-1}) P(y_1^{T-1}, q_1^{T-1})$$

$$= P(y_T | q_T, y_1^{T-1}, q_1^{T-1}) P(q_T | y_1^{T-1}, q_1^{T-1}) P(y_1^{T-1}, q_1^{T-1})$$

$$= P(y_T | q_T) P(q_T | q_{T-1}) P(y_1^{T-1}, q_1^{T-1})$$

When it is further factored, it becomes

$$= P(q_1) \prod_{t=2}^{T} P(q_t | q_{t-1}) \prod_{t=1}^{T} P(y_t | q_t)$$

In the above expressions,

- $P(q_1)$ is the initial state probability distribution of $q$ at a given time 1
- $P(q_t | q_{t-1})$ Is the probability of $q$ at time $t$ given $q$ at a given time $t+1$
- $P(y_t | q_t)$ is the emission probability

Let us use a real-life example to illustrate how computations of Markov chains can be done.

Suppose there are three places to eat in a small town. Now, two restaurants one Chinese while the second one is a Mexican restaurant. The third place is the pizza place. Everyone in this city can eat dinner in one of the three locations or can have a dinner at his/her home.

Assuming that 20% of those people who eat in the Chinese restaurant always go to the Mexican place next time, 20% who eat at home, and 30% will go to pizza place. From those people that eat in a Mexican restaurant, 10% will go to the pizza place, 25% will go to the Chinese restaurant, and 25%will eat at home next time.

From those who eat at home, 25% will go to a Mexican place, and 30% will go to pizza place. We call this situation a Markov system. This is because we are presented with four states (Chinese Restaurant, Mexican Restaurant, Pizza and Home). We are also presented with the probabilities of transitioning from one state to another.

A person in that town can eat dinner in any one of the places, where each of them forms a state. In this example, the Markov system has four states. We are interested in the success of these places regarding their business. For instance, after a given period, what is the percentage of people in the town that will go to the pizza place?

Suppose there is a mathematical system with k possible states and that any given one time, the system is in one and only one of the k states. Now, suppose that at any given observation period (say $n^{th}$ period), the likelihood of the system being in a specific state depends on its status at its n-1 period. Such as system is called a Markov chain or Markov process.

Since there are four states for the system, we can define $a_{ij}$ to be the probability of the scheme to be in state i with the previous state being j (at any given observation). The matrix $A = a_{ij}$ is called the transition matrix of the Markov Chain. Based on our description, the transition matrix will be:

```
.25   .20   .30   .2
.20   .30   .25   .2
.25   .20   .40   .1
.30   .30   .10   .2
```

In the matrix, the first column represents the state of eating at home, the second column shows the state of eating at the Chinese restaurant, the third column indicates the state of eating at the Mexican restaurant, and the fourth column indicates the state of eating at the Pizza Place. On the same note, the rows show eating at home, at the Chinese restaurant, at the Mexican restaurant and eating at the Pizza Place.

Let's summarize the expression as follows:

|  H  |  C  |  M  |  P  |
|------|------|------|------|
| .25 | .20 | .30 | .? |
| .20 | .30 | .25 | .? |
| .25 | .20 | .40 | .1 |
| .30 | .30 | .10 | .? |

Note though, that the sum of each column in the matrix is one. Any matrix that has this property is called a stochastic matrix or a Markov matrix. We want to answer the following question: What is the probability that the Markov system is in the $n$th state, at the $n$th observation?

For us to answer this question, we must first define the state vector. For any Markov Chain that has k states, the state vector for observation with period n is a column vector that is usually defined by:

$$X(n) = \begin{bmatrix} ? \\ ? \\ \\ ? \end{bmatrix}$$

Where $X_1 + X_2 + ...X_k$ is called a probability vector. From our example, if everyone eats at home, then the initial state vector $x^o$ is:

$$X0 = \begin{bmatrix} \quad \end{bmatrix}$$

In the next observation period (say at the end of the first week) the state vector will be:

$$X1 = A(X0) = \begin{bmatrix} .? \\ .? \\ .? \\ .? \end{bmatrix}$$

At the end of the second week, the state vector will become:

$$X^2 = A\left(X^1\right) = A\left(A\left(X^0\right)\right) = A^2X\left(^0\right)$$

From the above expression, we can now compute any probability that the Markov system is in the $n^{th}$ state, at the $n^{th}$ observation. The resulting computations indicate that the Markov system oscillates without approaching any fixed vector.

# Hidden Markov Models

A Hidden Markov Model (HMM is any statistical Markov model where the system being modeled is assumed to have a Markov process with unobserved or hidden states. HMMs can be presented as a dynamic Bayesian network where the system has states, transitional matrix, and the hidden states.

In other words, the HMM presents you with a system where you can observe a sequence of states, but don't know the sequence of the states that the model went through to generate the given states. Any HMM will always seek to recover the sequence of states from observed data.

As an example, let's consider a Markov model that has two states and six possible transitions. Assume the model uses:

- A red die that has six sides labeled 1 to 6.
- A green die that has twelve sides, five of them are marked 2 to 6, while the remaining seven have sides labeled 1.
- A weighted red coin where the probability of the heads is 0.9 and the probability of the tails is 0.1.
- A weighted green coin where the probability of heads is 0.95 while the probability of the tails is 0.05.

Now, the model creates a sequence of numbers from the set {1, 2, 3, 4, 5, and 6} with the following sets of rules: start by tossing up the red die and write down the number that comes up, which is the transition.

Roll the red coin and perform one of the following:

- When the result is headed, toss the red die and write down the outcome.
- When the result is tails, throw the green die and write down the outcome.
- At each successive step, flip the coin that has the same color as the die that you rolled in the previous step. When the coin comes up heads, toss the same die as in the previous step. If the coin comes up with tails, switch to the other die.

The state diagram for this Markov model that has two states (red and green) is shown in the following figure:

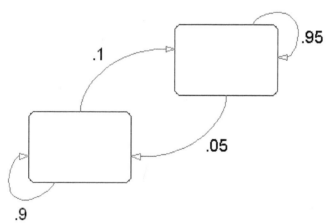

You can determine the transition from a state by tossing the die with the same color as the previous state. You can also find out the shift to the next state by flipping the coin with the same color as the original state.

The transition matrix is:

0.9    0

0.05   .9

The above model is not hidden because you already know the sequence of states from the colors of the coins and the dice. Suppose that someone wants to generate the transitions without showing you the dice or the coins. All you will see is the sequence of transitions. When you begin seeing more ones than other numbers, you may suspect that the Markov model is in the green state. However, you can't be sure since you cannot see the color of the die that is being rolled.

HMMs raise the following questions:

- Given any sequence of transitions, what is the most likely state path?
- Given any sequence of transition, how can you estimate the transition probabilities of the model?
- What is the forward probability that the Markov model will generate a given sequence?
- What is the posterior probability that the Markov model is in a particular state at any point in the sequence?

Three Markov problems are very useful in many application areas. These are:

- The evaluation problem. The evaluation problem can be used to find the probabilities of the observation given any sequence and the model. The solution of this problem can measure how well the model matches the observation sequence.
- The decoding problem. Given the model and the sequence, we can now determine the optimal state sequence of a system. The solution to this problem can solve word segmentation problem such as classification problems.
- The learning problem. If there is an existing model, we can use the technique to determine the model for the sequence and re-apply the same series for the learning and decoding complex problems.

# Mathematical definition of Markov models

A Hidden Markov Model (HMM) is merely a probabilistic function of the Markov property that we learned in the previous chapter. The term "hidden" shows that the system is a stochastic process where the state $q_1^t = \{q_1, \cdots\cdots, q_t\}$ of the Markov process is not directly observed (thus the term, "hidden"). However, it is implicitly defined by the sequence $y_1^t = \{y_1, \cdots\cdots, y_t\}$ of the observed data that doesn't necessarily exhibit the Markov property.

An HMM can be defined by the following conditional probabilities:

Given the variable $q_t$, the distribution of $y_t$ which is independent of every other variable, then

$$P\left(y_t \mid q_1^t, y_1^{t-1}\right) = P\left(y_t \mid q_t\right)$$

If $y_t$ is unable to affect $q_t$ given its history, then, we'll have:

$$P\left(q_{t+1} \mid q_1^t, y_1^t\right) = P\left(q_{t+1} \mid q_t\right)$$

Without the HMM assumptions, we'll not be in a position to compute the conditional probability because it would be intractable if all the history is to be considered.

To find the probability of the observed sequence, we'll apply the following formula in a recursive manner:

$$
\begin{aligned}
P\left(y_1^T, q_1^T\right) &= P\left(y_T, q_T \mid y_1^{T-1}, q_1^{T-1}\right) P\left(y_1^{T-1}, q_1^{T-1}\right) \\
&= P\left(y_T \mid q_T, y_1^{T-1}, q_1^{T-1}\right) P\left(q_T \mid y_1^{T-1}, q_1^{T-1}\right) P\left(y_1^{T-1}, q_1^{T-1}\right) \\
&= P\left(y_T \mid q_T\right) P\left(q_T \mid q_{T-1}\right) P\left(y_1^{T-1}, q_1^{T-1}\right)
\end{aligned}
$$

When it is further factored, it becomes

$$= P(q_1) \prod_{t=2}^{T} P(q_t | q_{t-1}) \prod_{t=1}^{T} P(y_t | q_t)$$

In the above expressions,

- $P(q_1)$ is the initial state probability distribution of $q$ at a given time 1
- $P(q_t | q_{t-1})$ Is the probability of $q$ at time $t$ given $q$ at a given time $t+1$
- $P(y_t | q_t)$ is the transition probability

## Forward recursion in HMM

As the name suggest, forward recursion computes $P(y_1^t, q_t)$ which is the probability of the observed partial sequence $y_1^t$ for any given state $q_t$. We can rewrite this joint probability as the conditional probability in the following product form:

$$P(y_1^t, q_t) = P(y_t | y_1^{t-1}, q_t) P(y_1^{t-1}, q_t)$$

According to HMM assumptions, the term $P(y_t | y_1^{t-1}, q_t)$ can be minimized to $P(y_t | q_t)$. Therefore, we'll have to compute $P(y_1^t, q_1^{t-1})$ to complete the equation.

$$
\begin{aligned}
P(y_1^t, q_t, q_{t-1}) &= P(q_t | q_{t-1}, y_1^{t-1}) P(y_1^{t-1}, q_{t-1}) \\
&= P(q_t | q_{t-1}) P(y_1^{t-1}, q_{t-1})
\end{aligned}
$$

The above expression is derived from HMM assumptions, When it is marginalized, it becomes:

$$P(y_1^{t-1}, q_t) = \sum_{q_{t-1}} P(y_1^t, q_t, q_{t-1})$$

$$= \sum_{q_{t-1}} P(q_t|q_{t-1}) P(y_1^{t-1}, q_{t-1})$$

Therefore, we obtain the following equation:

$$P(y_1^t, q_t) = P(y_t|q_t) \sum_{q_{t-1}} P(q_t|q_{t-1}) P(y_1^{t-1}, q_{t-1})$$

The above equation exhibits a recurrence relation so that the expression $P(y_1^t, q_t)$ can now be calculated recursively in a forward manner. We can now define $\alpha_q(t) = P(y_1^t, q)$ that can be expressed $\alpha_q(t) = P(y_t|Q_t = q) \sum_r (Q_t = q|Q_{t-1} = r) \alpha_r(t-1)$

Where $Q_t$ is the state space at a given time $t$

Forward recursions can be used to model a variety of systems. From the system, there will be an unlabeled sequence of observations O and a group of potential hidden states Q. Thus, for any given task, we would begin with a sequence of observations O = {1, 3, 2,...,} and the set of all the hidden states H and C. if you are generating an automatic text from part of a speech then you can start with a series of word observations O = {w1, w2, w3 ...} and a set of all the hidden states that corresponds to parts of the Speech Noun, the Verb, the Adjective and so on.

The standard protocol for HMM training is the Baum-Welch Welch algorithm which is a particular case of the Expectation-Maximization (EM) algorithm. The EM algorithm will allow you to train both the transition probability matrices A and the emission probability matrices B of the HMM. Of utmost importance to note about the EM is that it is an iterative algorithm.

Therefore, it works by calculating an initial estimate of all the probabilities. It then uses these estimates to compute a better estimate. The process repeats itself until the system improves on all the probabilities. By improving on the probabilities, the system is in a better position to learn from mistakes and improve.

For illustration, let us start by considering a much simpler case of training a Markov chain system rather than the HMM. Because the states in the Markov chain are observed, you can run the model on the observation series and directly observe which path you will take through the model and which state is generated during each observation symbol.

Obviously, a Markov chain system has no emission probabilities.Because of this, you can view the chain and degenerate the Markov where all the probabilities are 1.0 for the observed symbols and 0 for other symbols that are not observed. By doing this, we only need to train the transition probability matrices and not the emission matrices. You can also count the number of times the transition was taken by obtaining the maximum likelihood estimate of the probabilities.

## What about the backward recursion?

The backward recursion computes the partial probability from the time $t+1$ to the end of the sequence given ($q_t$). This can be expressed as follows:

$$P\left(y_{t+1}^T \middle| q_t\right) = \sum_{q_{t+1}} P\left(q_{t+1}, y_{t+1}, y_{t+2}^T \middle| q_t\right)$$

$$= \sum_{q_{t+1}} P\left(y_{t+2}^T \middle| q_{t+1}, y_{t+1}, q_t\right) P\left(y_{t+1} \middle| q_{t+1}, q_t\right) P\left(q_{t+1}, q_t\right)$$

$$P\left(y_{t+1}^T \middle| q_t\right) = \sum_{q_{t+1}} P\left(q_{t+1}, y_{t+1}, y_{t+2}^T \middle| q_t\right)$$

$$= \sum_{q_{t+1}} P\left(y_{t+2}^T | q_{t+1}, y_{t+1}, q_t\right) P\left(y_{t+1} | q_{t+1}, q_t\right) P\left(q_{t+1}, q_t\right)$$

From the above expression, you can note that $P\left(y_{t+1}^T | q_t\right)$ can only be computed once we have the information about $P\left(y_{t+2}^T | q_{t+1}\right)$. This is also known as backward recursion.

In particular, we can define $\beta_q(t) = P\left(y_{t+1}^T | Q_t = q\right)$, where the above equation can be expressed as follows:

$$\beta_q(t) = \sum_r \beta_r(t+1) P\left(y_{t+1} | Q_{t+1} = r\right) P\left(Q_{t+1} = r | Q_t = q\right)$$

In the above expression, $Q_t$ is the state at a given time $t$

## How to select the best state sequence

At the outset, choosing the best state sequence means finding the most likely state sequence $q_1^T$ that corresponds to a given observation sequence $y_1^T$. Now, since our primary interest is in the overall performance of the model rather than determining a specific sequence, we can use an approach that maximizes the expected number of states the HMMs.

The state posterior probability $P\left(q_t | y_1^T\right)$ which is the probability of being in a particular state at a given time t, given the observation sequence $y_1^T$ can be expressed using variables that we have already defined from the previous forward and backward chains.

The probability $P\left(q_t | y_1^T\right)$ is the product of the forward-backward variables and can be normalized by the joint distribution of the observation sequences. Therefore, we can express it in the following manner:

$$P\left(q_t \mid y_1^T\right) = \frac{P\left(q_t, y_1^T\right)}{P\left(y_1^T\right)}$$

$$= \frac{P\left(y_1^t \mid q_t\right) P\left(q_t\right) P\left(y_{t+1}^T \mid q_t\right)}{P\left(y_1^T\right)} = \frac{P\left(y_1^t, q_t\right) P\left(y_{t+1}^T \mid q_t\right)}{P\left(y_1^T\right)}$$

Because $P\left(q_t \mid y_1^T\right)$ is already normalized by the joint probabilities of the observation sequences, the resulting expression will be:

$$\sum P\left(q_t \mid y_1^T\right) = 1$$

From this, we can conclude that the most likely state which will be measured by maximizing $P\left(q_t \mid y_1^T\right)$ and therefore selecting the best state sequence is $q_t$.

## HMM in real-life situations

A very effective and perceptive way to figure out the application of HMM is in sequential pattern recognition tasks, such as speech recognition systems, protein sequence analysis systems, machine translation systems and many others.

Let's have a real-world example of applying HMM in Markov logic to perform segmentation of the transport systems.

Suppose that on a given day you observe a car taking three actions: either stopped, driving, or slowing. Now assume that this is only dependent on the state of the stoplight which is in front of it: either red, green or yellow. In a Markov system, you'll need to model the rules and observations at specific points in time.

Here is a summary of what you have so far:

```
State = {Stop, Drive, Slow}
Observations = {Red, Green, Yellow}
Time = {0... 10}
```

This can be summarized as follows:

```
State (state, time)
Observation (observation, time)
```

In the Markov logic, you need to express some constraints that are inherent to HMMs explicitly. In particular, you should state that at each given time step there is exactly one state and observation. Let's use the! Operator to specify this observation. We'll have the following state space and transition system:

```
State(s! t)
Observation (observation! ,t)
```

Now, we should find the probability of transition and observation for each state and its successor. Also, we should also determine the prior probability of each state at the beginning point. These probabilities can be summarized as follows:

```
State (+s, 0)
State (+s1, t) => State (+s2, t+1)
Observations (+o, t) => State (+s, t)
```

By using the + operator, we are generating a clause for each stat and observation for each state pair. This allows you to learn the weights for each of the combinations. We can learn weights from the data by using such a system.

# Chapter 4: Implementation of Markov Models in Python Programming

When Guido van Rossum developed Python programming language in the late 1980s, little did he know that the language will be more famous than popular programming languages in machine learning and Artificial Intelligence. The fact is—in the last couple of years; the Python language has emerged as a solution for most machine learning problems.

Python language is beginner-friendly, yet very powerful. It is no wonder that Python language is finding its applications in some of the most popular organizations such as Google, Pinterest, Mozilla, Survey Monkey, Slideshare, YouTube, and Reddit as a core developer language. Also, Python's syntax is extremely simple to understand and follow if you're a beginner or advanced programmer.

If you're an advanced developer of C, C++, Java or Perl, you'll find the advanced part of programming in Python to be simple. If you're an experienced developer, you can accomplish great things with Python. Besides developing games, data analysis, and machine learning, Python language can also be used to code general AI systems and development of GUIs.

This chapter explores how you can implement Markov models in Python language. Without further ado, let's get started.

## Getting started with Python

To implement Markov models in Python, you need to install it on your computer and set the programming environment. If you're a novice Python programmer, learning basics of Python installation and setting up the environment will go a long way in promoting your bottom line.

# The installation process

The process of downloading and installing the Python language interpreter is pretty simple. If you're using the latest Linux distribution—whether it's Ubuntu, Fedora or Mint—then you'll find the most recent version of Python already installed. All you have to do is to update your system.

If you're using a Debian-based Linux distribution, follow these steps to update your system:

- Launch the Terminal app and type the following command at the command prompt:

```
su apt-get update
```

- Type your root password and press the Enter key
- Wait for the update process to be completed.

If you're using a Redhat-based Linux distribution such as Fedora, follow these steps to update your system:

- Launch the Terminal app and type the following command at the command prompt:

```
su apt-get update
```

- Type your root password and press the Enter key
- Wait for the update process to be completed.

On the other hand, if you're using other OS's apart from Linux, you have to download and install Python yourself.

If you're using an older version of Linux that has no Python, then you have to install it manually.

Follow the steps outlined below to install Python on Linux distributions:

- Launch the Terminal app (Ensure that you're connected to the internet)
- Type "su" at the command prompt and press the enter key
- Type your root password and hit the enter key
- If you're using Debian-based Linux distribution such as Ubuntu, then type: "apt-get install python" at the command prompt and press the enter key
- On the other hand, if you're using the Red Hat/ RHEL / CentOS Linux distributions such as Fedora, then type: "yum install python" at the command prompt and hit the Enter key.
- Wait for the installation to complete.
- Update the system by typing: "su apt-get update" if you're using Debian-based Linux distributions or "su yum update" if you're a Redhat/ RHEL / CentOS Linux distribution user.

### *What about Windows OS?*

Before you download and install Python, decide on the version of Python language that you would want to install. As a rule of thumb, always go for the latest version. At the time of writing this book, the latest version was 3.6.1. Here are steps that can help you install Python on Windows OS:

- Go to www.python.org and download the current version of Python. Select the appropriate version depending on the nature of your OS (32 bit, or 64 bit).
- Open the Python file that you've just downloaded

- Click on the "Accept the default settings" from the on-screen instructions and wait for the installation process to complete.

If you're a Mac OS X or Sierra user, then you'll find Python 2.7 already ported to the OS. Therefore, you don't have to install or configure anything if you want to begin using Python. However, if you wish to install the latest version of Python, you need to use the Homebrew. Here are steps that can help install Python on your Mac OS:

- Open your Terminal or any of your favorite OSX terminal emulator
- Type the following command at the command prompt: "/user/bin/ruby-e"$(curl-fsSL https://raw.githubusercontent.com/Homebrew/install/master/install)".
- Wait for the app to be installed.
- Once the installation process has completed, insert the Homebrew directory at the top of the PATH environment variable. You can perform this operation by adding the following line at the bottom of the "~/.profile" file: "export PATH=/usr/local/bin: /usr/local/sbin: $PATH"
- Now proceed to install Python language interpreter by typing the following command at the command prompt: "brew install python."
- Wait for the installation process to complete.

Now that you've installed Python, what next?

Obviously, it's now time to begin programming. But not that fast! You should decide on what text editor you'll use. You can opt to select your best editors to help you code and execute your program. Some of the most popular Text Editors are Emacs, Geany, Komodo Edit and Sublime Text.

But since we all know the pitfalls of the Text Editors—such as running the code manually from the Python Shell—I won't advise you to use them. Instead, use the Python IDLE (Integrated Development Environment). I have been using it ever since without problems. However, you can choose an IDE that suits you.

Python IDLE has the following features:

- Syntax highlighting
- Auto-completion of code statements
- Smart indentation
- Integrated debugger with the stepping, persistent breakpoints, and call stack visibility features.

Next up, let's now explore Python packages that are useful in machine learning.

## Python Packages for machine learning

To be acquainted with Python data analysis libraries, you must first understand how mathematical libraries work in Python. Ultimately, the first step is learning how to import them into your programming environment. You can use:

```
import math as ml
```

Or

```
from math import *
```

In the first code, we have defined an alias `ml` to the Python library "`math`." You can now proceed to use various functions from the math library such as factorial by referencing it using its alias `t.factorial()`. In the second code, we have just imported the entire namespace in for Python library "math, " and we can directly use `factorial()` without referring to the math library.

Below are common machine learning libraries that you'll find in Python:

## #1: Tensorflow

Tensorflow is the newest neural network library—developed for the Google Brain Project—that has just been released. It is a high-level neural network Python package that helps machine learning programmers to code network architectures while providing abstraction.

## #2: Scikit-learn

The scikit-learn library is undeniably one of, if not the most, popular machine learning libraries. It has numerous features for data mining and analysis making it a definite choice for most machine learning programmers. It's developed on top of the popular NumPy, SciPy, and the Matplotlib libraries. Therefore, you have to be familiar with NumPy, SciPy and Matplotlib libraries if you want to exploit its machine learning potentials.

## #4: Theano

Theano is a machine learning package that allows machine learning programmers to define, optimize, and evaluate mathematical expressions that involve multi-dimensional arrays. Just like Scikit-learn, Theano is built on top of NumPy. Because it makes use GPU in a transparent manner, Theano applications are fast and easy to set up.

# #4: Pylearn2

Most of the Pylearn2's functionality is built on top of the Theano library, so it has a pretty solid base. It provides the flexibility that machine learning programmers can get while coding their systems. Pylearn2 can also wrap with other machine learning libraries such as the Scikit-learn to provide systems that produce excellent results.

# #5: Pyevolve

One of the more interesting and different areas of neural network research remains the space of genetic algorithms. These algorithms test a neural network on data that they have to provide feedback on the performance and fitness functionalities. Networks that have higher fitness scores win out and are then applied to the parent to the new generations. Pyevolve provides an excellent framework that can build and execute genetic algorithms.

# #6: NuPIC

NuPIC is a machine learning library that is based on the theory of the neocortex that is commonly called the Hierarchical Temporal Memory (HTM). HTMs are hierarchical, time-based memory systems that can be trained on various types' data. These frameworks are used to mimic how the human memory and computation are intertwined within the brain.

Now that you've learned the most popular machine learning libraries let's dive in to implement HMM in Python language.

## Implementing HMM algorithms in Python

We have so far learned that HMM is generative probabilistic models where a sequence of observable variables are generated by a series of internal states that are hidden that you can't observe directly. The transitions between the hidden states are assumed to take the Markov chain systems. We've also learned that Markov chains can be specified by a start probability vector and the transition probability vector.

The emission probability of any observable event can be any probability distribution that is conditioned on the current hidden state. Therefore, HMM can entirely be defined by the start probability vector, transition probability matrix, and the emission probability. For you to implement any HMM system, you have to understand how the three parameters will work.

Even before you can begin to implement HMMs in Python, you should first identify the fundamental challenges for HMMs. There are three basic challenges for HMMs:

- Given the model parameters and the observed data, how can you estimate the optimal sequence of hidden states?
- Given the model parameters and the observed data, how can you compute the probability of the data?
- Given just the observed data, how can you estimate the model parameters?

The first and the second problem can easily be solved by two dynamic programming algorithms –Viterbi algorithm and the Forward-Backward algorithm—respectively. The third problem can be solved by using the iterative Expectation-Maximization (EM) algorithm that is also called Baum-Welch algorithm.

To implement these algorithms, we'll use hmmlearn.

# hmmlearn

hmmlearn is a set of algorithms that can implement Hidden Markov Models.

For you to use hmmlearn, you need the following dependencies:

- Python version 2.6 or higher
- NumPy
- SciPy
- Scikit-learn

There are currently three models available for hmmlearn. These are:

- hmm.GaussianHMM. It is the HMM that is used with Gaussian emissions.
- hmm.GMMHMM. It is HMM that we use with Gaussian mixture emissions.
- hmm.MultinomialHMM. It is HMM that is used with multinomial (discrete) emissions

To install hmmlearn, ensure you have installed all the dependencies that I have listed above. Then type the following command and run it:

```
pip install -U --user hmmlearn
```

Next, let's explore how you can now implement HMM in Python.

# How to build HMM and generate samples

You can build an HMM instance by passing the arguments described above (hmm.GaussianHMM, hmm.GMMHMM, hmm.MultinomialHMM) to the constructor. After that, you can begin to generate samples from HMM by calling sample. Here's an illustration:

```
import numpy as np
from hmmlearn import hmm
np.random.seed(42)
mymodel = hmm.GaussianHMM(n_components=3,
covariance_type= "full")
mymodel.startprob_ = np.array([0.6, 0.3, 0.1])
mymodel.transmat_ = np.array([[0.7, 0.2, 0.1],
...                             [0.3, 0.5, 0.2],
...                             [0.3, 0.3, 0.4]])
mymodel.means_ = np.array([[0.0, 0.0], [3.0, -
3.0], [5.0, 10.0]])
mymodel.covars_ = np.tile(np.identity(2), (3, 1,
1))
X, Z = mymodel.sample(100).
```

The transitional probability matrix need not to be automatic. For example, the left-right HMM can be specified as follows:

```
lrhmm = hmm.GaussianHMM(n_components=3,
covariance_type= "diag",
...                      init_params= "cm",
params= "cmt")
>>> lrhmm.startprob_ = np.array([1.0, 0.0, 0.0])
>>> lrhmm.transmat_ = np.array([[0.5, 0.5, 0.0],
...                             [0.0, 0.5, 0.5],
...                             [0.0, 0.0, 1.0]])
```

*How can you fix the parameters?*

Each HMM argument has a character code that you can use to customize its initialization and estimation. The emission algorithm should have a starting point to proceed. Therefore, before the training process, each parameter should be assigned a value in a random manner, or it can be computed from the data.

To fix the parameters, ensure that the character code of the argument is missing from the init_params and set the parameter its desired value.

For instance, consider a HMM that has explicitly initialized transition probability matrix below:

```
mymodel = hmm.GaussianHMM(n_components=3,
n_iter=100, init_params= "mcs")
mymodel.transmat_ = np.array([[0.7, 0.2, 0.1],
...                            [0.3, 0.5, 0.2],
...                            [0.3, 0.3, 0.4]])
```

Do you want to see a quick sampling process in action? Well, here's a Python script that demonstrates to sample points from HMM. It uses 4 components with defined mean and covariance. The resulting plot should show a sequence of observations generated with the transitions.

```
print (__doc__)
import numpy as np
import matplotlib.pyplot as myplot
from hmmlearn import hmm
#Prepare the parameters for a 4-components HMM
population probability distribution
starting = np.array([0.6, 0.3, 0.1, 0.0])
# The transition probability matrix. You can note
that there are transitions.
# Between the components 1 and 3
transmatrix = np.array([[0.7, 0.2, 0.0, 0.1],
                        [0.3, 0.5, 0.2, 0.0],
                        [0.0, 0.3, 0.5, 0.2],
                        [0.2, 0.0, 0.2, 0.6]])
```

```python
# The means for each of the components
means = np.array([[0.0,  0.0],
                  [0.0, 11.0],
                  [9.0, 10.0],
                  [11.0, -1.0]])
# The covariance for each of the component
covariance = .5 * np.tile(np.identity(2), (4, 1,
1))
# Building an HMM instance and setting the
parameters
mymodel = hmm.GaussianHMM(n_components=4,
covariance_type="full")
# Instead of fitting it from data, you directly
set the estimated
# Parameters, their means and covariance of the
various components
mymodel.starting_ = starting
mymodel.transmatrix_ = transmatrix
mymodel.means_ = means
mymodel.covars_ = covariance
# Generating the samples
X, Z = mymodel.sample(500)
# plotting the sampled data
myplot.plot(X[:, 0], X[:, 1], ".-",
label="observations", ms=6,
        mfc="orange", alpha=0.7)
# Indicating the component numbers
for i, m in enumerate(means):
    myplot.text(m[0], m[1], 'Component %i' % (i +
1),
            size=17,
horizontalalignment='center',
            bbox=dict(alpha=.7, facecolor='w'))
myplot.legend(loc='best')
# Displaying the output
myplot.show()
```

# How to train HMM parameters and infer hidden states

You can train any HMM system by calling the fit method. Your input data is a matrix of concatenated sequences of observations—or the samples—along with the lengths of the sequences. Note though, that since the EM algorithm is a gradient-based optimization system, it will get stuck in the local optima.

Therefore, you should try to run the fit method with various initializations and then select the highest scored model. The score of the model can then be computed by the scoring method. The inferred optimal hidden states are obtained by calling the predict method. You'll specify the predict method using a decoder algorithm. Currently, the Viterbi algorithm and the maximum a posteriori estimation or map are supported.

Here's an example code:

```
trainmodel = hmm.GaussianHMM(n_components=3,
covariance_type= "full", n_iter=100)
trainmodel.fit(X)
GaussianHMM(algorithm='viterbi',...
Z2 = trainmodel.predict(X)
```

To monitor convergence in HMM, you should find out the number of EM iterations. The number of EM algorithm iterations is usually upper bounded by the n_iter parameter. The training will proceed until the n_iter steps have been performed, or the change of score is lower than the defined threshold tol.However, depending on the training data, the EM algorithm may or may not achieve the convergence in the given number of steps.

The monitor_ attribute can be used to diagnose convergence in such cases. Here's an example:

```
remodel.monitor_
ConvergenceMonitor(history=[...],
          iter=15, n_iter=200, tol=0.01,
verbose=False)
remodel.monitor_.converged
True
```

To pass multiple sequences of data for fitness and predict, we must first concatenate them into a single array and then calculate an array of sequence lengths. Here's an example:

```
g = np.concatenate([g1, g2])
lengthg = [len(g1), len(g2)]
```

Finally, just call the desired method with g and lengthsg. Here's an example:

```
hmm.GaussianHMM(n_components=3).fit(g, lengthg)
GaussianHMM(algorithm= "Viterbi", ...
```

Below is an example of Python script that can help you understand how training is done. The Python script demonstrates how to use the Gaussian HMM on the stock price data from Yahoo! finance.

```
from __future__ import print_function
import datetime
import numpy as np
from matplotlib import cm, pyplot as myplot
from matplotlib.dates import YearLocator,
MonthLocator
try:
    from matplotlib.finance import
yahoo_historical_yahoo_ochl
except for ImportError:
    # For the Matplotlib before 1.5 version.
    from matplotlib.finance import (
        yahoo_historical_yahoo as
yahoo_historical_yahoo_ochl
```

```
    )
from hmmlearn.hmm import GaussianHMM
print(__doc__)
#Getting yahoo from Yahoo! Finance site
yahoo = yahoo_historical_yahoo_ochl(
    "INTC", datetime.date(1995, 1, 1),
datetime.date(2012, 1, 6))

# Unpack yahoo
dates = np.array([q[0] for q in yahoo], dtype=int)
close_v = np.array([q[2] for q in yahoo])
volume = np.array([q[5] for q in yahoo])[1:]
# Taking the difference of close value. Note,
though that this makes
# the``len(diff) = len(close_t) - 1``, therefore,
other quantities also
# should to be shifted by 1.
difference = np.difference(close_v)
dates = dates[1:]
close_v = close_v[1:]
# Pack diff and volume for training.
X = np.column_stack([diff, volume])
#Running the Gaussian HMM
print("fitting to HMM and decoding ...", end="")
# Make an HMM instance and execute fit
mymodel = GaussianHMM(n_components=4,
covariance_type="diag", n_iter=1000).fit(X)
# Predict the optimal sequence of internal hidden
state
hidden_states = model.predict(X)
print("done")
#Out:
#Fitting to the HMM and decoding ...done
#Print the trained parameters and plot
print("Transition matrix")
print(model.transmat_)
print()
```

```
print("The Means and variance of each hidden
state")
for i in range(model.n_components):
    print("{0}th the hidden state". Format(i))
    print("mean = ", model.means_[i])
    print("var = ", np.diag(model.covars_[i]))
    print()
fig, axs = myplot.subplots(model.n_components,
sharex=True, sharey=True)
colours = cm.rainbow(np.linspace(0, 1,
model.n_components))
for i, (ax, colour) in enumerate(zip(axs,
colours)):
#Use the fancy indexing to plot the data in each
state.
    mask = hidden_states == i
    ax.plot_date(dates[mask], close_v[mask], ".-",
c=colour)
    ax.set_title("{0}th hidden state".format(i))
    # Formatting the ticks.
    ax.xaxis.set_major_locator(YearLocator())
    ax.xaxis.set_minor_locator(MonthLocator())
    ax.grid(True)
myplot.show()
```

# How to save and load HMM

After training, HMM can be easily continued for future use with the pickle module. Or, you can use the more efficient joblib package. Here's an example:

```
from sklearn.externals import joblib
joblib.dump(remodel, "filename.pkl")
["filename.pkl"]
joblib.load("filename.pkl")
GaussianHMM(algorithm="Viterbi",...
```

## How to implement HMMs using custom emission probabilities

If you want to implement custom emission probabilities such as Poisson distributions, you have to subclass the _BaseHMM and override the following methods:

- base._BaseHMM._init(X, lengths). It initializes the model parameters before the fitting process.
- base._BaseHMM._check (). It validates the model parameters before the fitting process.
- base._BaseHMM._generate_sample_from_state (state). It produces a random sample of any given component.
- base._BaseHMM._compute_log_likelihood(X). It calculates per-component log probability in the model.
- base._BaseHMM._initialize_sufficient_statistics (). It initializes the sufficient statistics that are required for M-step.
- base._BaseHMM._accumulate_sufficient_statistics (…). It updates sufficient statistics from any given sample.
- base._BaseHMM._do_mstep (stats). It performs the M-step of the EM algorithm.

# Chapter 5: Applications of HMMs

Although conceived in the 1960s and 1970s as statistical models, HMMs have become increasingly popular in recent times. There are 2 primary reasons for this growth. First, HMMs are rich in mathematical concepts and thus forms an excellent theoretical background in a majority of machine learning applications.

Second, when applied rightly, HMMs provides a robust, practical implementation framework for most complex machine learning problems. In this chapter, we review some of the applications of HMMs in real-life situations. Let's get started.

## Gaming

Game theory is by far the most commonly used framework to model various problems in economics and other fields. It continues to be utilized in a variety of applications such as computer science, biology, among others. The study of the game theory depends on describing, exhibiting and solving complex problems that are related to interactions between decision makers.

Markov models can be used to map rival player behaviors as a set of different states where each state has a predetermined payoff table. Suppose we are to model and implement a game G that is repeated in the first round the state of nature. Then Markov models can help us model the probability distribution p where only one player (say player 1) knows this state.

In the same game, another player (say player 2) knows the possible states but doesn't know the actual winning state. After each round of play, both players will know the action of each one and then play again. In this game, instead of the probability that is associated with the initial state of nature, Markov Chain Transition Probability Distribution can be used to model the system through time.

In such a case, both players will know the action of each other after each round, but only one player should be aware the actual and the past states and the payoff associated that is linked with those actions. We can say that player 2 knows the Transition Probability Distribution. This means that the transition between the types of player 1 has to adhere to the Markov Property.

Now, since player 2 doesn't know the state of player 1, you can't model and solve this problem using the stochastic game or Markov chain game. Fortunately, HMMs can come in at this time and help you model such a problem. The Hidden Markov Game should have the following elements:

- A finite set of players;
- All the strategies that players can employ in the game (strategy set);
- Type sets, one for each player;
- A set of transition functions;
- A finite set of observation state variables.
- The payoff functions;
- Probability Distribution that represents the players' prior belief about their opponents.

From the above components, a probability distribution that links each state of the Markov chain to the observable states should be modeled by transition matrix, and Baum-Welch Algorithm used to infer the HMM.

# Speech recognition

Hidden Markov Models (HMMs) are still by far the most powerful and flexible methods for representing and classifying data that has trends over a given time. HMMs have been an essential component of speech recognition systems for a long time now. You can quickly implement a speech recognition system by using the Gaussian Mixture Model HMM and GMM-HMM in NumPy package.

For you to implement this system, you need a dataset to operate on. For large datasets, the HMM can search for learning words in two basic steps. The first phase will generate a world lattice of the n-best phrase sequences that has a simple framework for calculating the approximate probabilities of sounds in real-time.

In the second phase, a more accurate probability is computed and compared with a limited number of hypotheses. The machine learning search continues until a single-word sequence is produced with only one step. A Gaussian Mixture Model HMM (GMM-HMM) can help model and implement such a system.

To demonstrate HMM in speech recognition, the code below can help you figure out the system can learn the various words. In the code, we have an audio file located at: http://www.saad.com/myaudio/HMM.mp3. You can substitute this URL with the exact location where your audio file is located.

```
import numpy as np
import matplotlib.pyplot as myplot
%matplotlib inline
from utils import progress_bar_downloader
import os
#The original file is here:
http://www.saad.com/myaudio/HMM.mp3.
link = "http://www.saad.com/myaudio/HMM.mp3"
```

```
filepaths = []
filelabels = []
spokenwords = []
for f in os.listdir('audio'):
    for w in os.listdir('audio/' + f):
        filepaths.append('audio/' + f + '/' + w)
    filelabels.append(f)
        if f not in spokenwords:
            spokenwords.append(f)
print('Words spoken:', spokenwords)
```

Now supposed the words are ['banana', 'apple', 'mango', 'lemon', 'orange', 'guava', 'pineapple'], then we'll have a total of 7 different spoken words. If each word is spoken 15 different times, then we'll end up with a grand total of 105 files. Such files should be extracted into a single data matrix and a label vector created. Here's how you can achieve this:

```
from scipy.io import wavfile
mydata = np.zeros((len(filepaths), 32000))
maxsize = -1
for n,file in enumerate(filepaths):
    _, d = wavfile.read(file)
    data[n, :d.shape[0]] = d
    if d.shape[0] > maxsize:
        maxsize = d.shape[0]
mydata = mydata[:, :maxsize]
#Each sample audio file is one row of data, and
has one entry in labels
print('Number of files total:', mydata.shape[0])
all_labels = np.zeros(data.shape[0])
for n, l in enumerate(set(labels)):
    all_labels[np.array([i for i, _ in
enumerate(labels) if _ == l])] = n
    print('Labels and label indices', all_labels)
```

Next, we can now implement the speech recognition system. Here's a code that can help you:

---

```
import matplotlib.pyplot as myplot
plt.myplot(data[0, :], color='steelblue')
plt.title('Timeseries example for
for%s'%labels[0])
myplot.xlim(0, 3500)
myplot.xlabel('Time (samples)')
myplot.ylabel('Amplitude (signed 16 bit)')
myplot.figure()
log_freq = 20 * np.log(np.abs(stft(xdata[0, :])) +
1)
print(log_freq.shape)
plt.imshow(log_freq, cmap='gray',
interpolation=None)
myplot.xlabel('Freq (bin)')
myplot.ylabel('Time (overlapped frames)')
myplot.ylim(log_freq.shape[1])
myplot.title('PSD of %s example'%labels[0])
```

## Random Text Generation

The realm of speech synthesis has evolved significantly during the past couple of years, due to as a result of fast-paced, ever-expanding and complex technologies such as cellular telephony systems. Amidst this growth, the most popular methods of speech synthesis have remained the HMMs. HMMs of order k can estimate the likelihood of occurrence of a given value at a particular position based on the sequence of characters that can constitute the learning process.

In these systems, the number of occurrences of words or phrases of length k can be computed, and the system can quickly estimate the probability of given words appearing in a sentence. HMMs can help model a system that automatically generates words from part-of-speech sequences. You can use HMM to train the system on sample words that you input. Once the words have been entered, the system can now generate sentences at random from the model. The system can also create test sentences and find the most likely hidden state sequences.

In summary, here are steps that a text generator in HMM can be modeled:

- Take any two consecutive words from the dataset. Build a chain of words where the last two words of the chain show the current state in the system.
- Check all the incidences of the last two words that are in the current state. If they appear more than once, then select one of them randomly and increment the word that follows them at the end of the chain.
- Repeat the preceding step until you've reached the desired length of the generated text.

Take a look at the code below for further illustration:

```
import sys
from pprint import pprint
from random import choice
EOS = ['.', '?', '!']
def build_dict(words):
#     Build a dictionary from the words.
#     (word1, word2) => [w1, w2,] # key: tuple;
value: list
    dict = {}
    for i, word in enumerate(words):
        try:
```

```python
            first, second, third = words[i],
words[i+1], words[i+2]
        except IndexError:
            break
        mykey = (first, second)
        if mykey not in dict:
            dict[mykey] = []
        #
        dict[mykey].append(third)
    return dict
def generate_sentence(dict):
    li = [key for key in dict.keys() if
key[0][0].isupper()]
    mykey = choice(li)
    li = []
    first, second = mykey
    li.append(first)
    li.append(second)
    while True:
        try:
            third = choice(d[mykey])
        except KeyError:
            break
        li.append(third)
        if third[-1] in EOS:
            break
        # else
        mykey = (second, third)
        first, second = mykey
    return ' '.join(li)
def main():
    filename = sys.argv[1]
    with open(filename, "rt", encoding="utf-8") as
f:
        mytext = filename.read()
    words = text.split()
    dict = build_dict(words)
```

```
        pprint(dict)
        print()
        sent = generate_sentence(dict)
        print(sent)
        if sent in mytext:
            print('# existing sentence :(')
if __name__ == "__main__":
    if len(sys.argv) == 1:
        print("Error: provide an input dataset
file.")
        sys.exit(1)
    # else
    main()
```

## Weather reporting

HMMs can help you model a system that extracts information from weather stations and report it directly to users. All you need is the pywapi API. You can easily download this API from the Google page. You can install it using pip, easy_install or manually with the command line. When you use the command line you have to use the setup.py.
Consider the Python script below:

```
import pywapi
weather_result =
pywapi.get_weather_from_weather_com("UKXX0085")
print ("The weather from weather.com says: It's "
+
weather_result["current_conditions"]["text"].lower
() + " and " +
weather_result['current_conditions']["temperature'
" + "°C now in New York.")
```

In the above code we have used the pywapi to implement a weather report system that displays the temperature and cloud conditions in New York.

If you want a more elaborate system that considers any part of the world, you can import the pywapi into your system and allow it prompt for a city from the user. Consider the Python script below:

```python
import pywapi

mycity = input("Enter the name of your city: ")
#This sets up a dictionary of all the cities in
the world with the city's name
lookup = pywapi.get_location_ids(city)
#workaround to access the last item of the
dictionary
for i in lookup:
    location_id = i
#location_id will now contain the city's code
weather_result =
pywapi.get_weather_from_weather_com(location_id)
print ("The weather from weather.com says: It's "
+
weather_result["current_conditions"]["text"].lower
() + " and " +
weather_result['current_conditions']["temperature'
" + "°C now in New York.")
```

# Conclusion

The primary aim of machine learning is to train the computers or machine to learn on its own and make informed decisions in a relatively shorter time than what human beings can do. While the promising applications of machine learning continue to grow daily, the time and effort required to train such optimized machine learning systems are substantial. Constant training and providing information isn't the natural way for these tools to learn and obtain the necessary knowledge.

All these dynamics point to the treasured potentials of unsupervised machine learning algorithms, which if done correctly can allow systems to learn and deduct mostly without the help of a human being. Today, you're likely to interact with all sorts of computer systems based on machine learning. From image recognition systems used on social media platforms to voice recognition systems used in personal assistants, the list of unsupervised machine learning keeps on expanding.

As the field grows further, the potentials of unsupervised machine learning will be revolutionary in both social and economic arena. Markov models—and specifically the HMMs—continues to inspire confidence among machine learning enthusiasts. HMMs are today providing support for complex problems that involves uncertainties in a continuous period. With the ever-increasing computing power, these models are likely to play an active role in the growth of machine learning applications.

The fact that you've read the entire contents of this book means that you're really interested machine learning and Markov models. Otherwise, if you were not, you wouldn't have wasted your precious time combing through this book. I am glad that you are keen on Markov models and machine learning.

Now, this is only the first step. Remember, you want to be a top-notch machine learning programmer. Top-notch machine learning developers don't give up along the way. Go ahead and practice to conceptualize all the ideas that you have learned in this book. Remember, the rule of thumb in learning anything is practice. And good practice makes perfect!

Do you have any burning questions regarding Markov models and unsupervised learning in Python? Share your concerns with us.

# Further Resources

Further resources on Markov models and unsupervised learning in Python can be obtained from the following sources:

1. https://www.sas.com/en_us/insights/analytics/machine-learning.html
2. http://www.kdnuggets.com/2016/08/10-algorithms-machine-learning-engineers.html
3. http://cdn.intechopen.com/pdfs/10694.pdf
4. http://disp.ee.ntu.edu.tw/~pujols/Machine%20Learning%20Tutorial.pdf
5. http://mlsso8.rsise.anu.edu.au/files/smola.pdf
6. http://www.ulb.ac.be/di/map/gbonte/mod_stoch/syl.pdf
7. http://scribd-download.com/essentials-of-machine-learning-algorithms-with-python-and-r-codes_58a2f7506454a7a940b1e8ec_pdf.html
8. http://machinelearningmastery.com/supervised-and-unsupervised-machine-learning-algorithms/
9. https://page.mi.fu-berlin.de/rojas/neural/chapter/K5.pdf
10. http://www.cs.upc.edu/~bejar/apren/docum/trans/09-clusterej-eng.pdf
11. http://webee.technion.ac.il/people/shimkin/LCS11/ch4_RL1.pdf
12. http://web.mst.edu/~gosavia/neural_networks_RL.pdf
13. https://web.stanford.edu/~jurafsky/slp3/9.pdf
14. https://wiki.inf.ed.ac.uk/twiki/pub/CSTR/TrajectoryModelling/HTS-Introduction.pdf
15. https://media.readthedocs.org/pdf/python/stable/python.pdf
16. http://www.cse.unt.edu/~tarau/teaching/NLP/HMM.pdf

www.ingramcontent.com/pod-product-compliance
Lightning Source LLC
LaVergne TN
LVHW052304060326
832902LV00021B/3690